Tim and Mike have made the most solid statement I've ever read on the *human condition* and ways to improve it for individuals and organizations. If you want to be a spark to ignite person and organization improvement then this book is for you.

—Dr. Robert C. Preziosi
Professor and Leadership and HR Management
Author, *The Leadership Road*

———————

Who knew that the recipe for a fresh and exciting approach to individual and organizational therapies involved the serendipitous blend of equal parts Irish Scamp and Island Boy? Tim and Mike's journey and commitment in writing this book highlights their insights into clinical work empowering people to write their own script. They engage us in their compassionate fervor to jolt awake societies and free them of prejudice towards Mental Illness. Wow, great read!!!!

—Pam Brown, LCSW, MSW, BCBA,
Pam Brown Counseling Services
—Ted Brown, Managing Broker,
Berkshire Hathaway HomeServices Florida Realty

———————

I0425989

Finally there is a book that goes beyond the regular cultural practices in the Bahamas. Doctors Timothy McCartney and Michael Neville use the fine art of professional collaboration to bring to the fore deep rooted cultural behaviors in the Bahamas that for many years have remained hidden. This latest effort by Doctors McCartney and Neville is told in anecdotal format so that everyone (particularly Bahamians) who reads this book comes away richer and more informed about the deeper aspects of Bahamian culture for having done so. I could not put the book down until I had read it from cover to cover…I am richer for the experience. Thank you Doctors McCartney and Neville. Bahamian culture will never be the same!

—Dr. Donald M. McCartney, D.M.
Former Educator/Senior Public Officer
Diplomat for the Commonwealth of the Bahamas

This is a fulfilling and holistic book on understanding basic concepts of human behavior in order to commence the healing process; a very good read and an excellent manual to enhance and redefine the new you.

—Oliver H. Jobson,
Author of ***Expanding the Boundaries of Self Beyond the Limit of Traditional Thought***

———————

U-Turn is an ideal read for the layman who is interested in mental health. Drs. Tim McCartney and Mike Neville explain the basics in mental health and their situational approach to cures for the respective diseases. It is a wonderful survey of their historical and modern day explanations of the world we live in. The book is laced with humor and anecdotes of their many years in practice in the Bahamas and Caribbean. Their impact on the Bahamas was and still is insurmountable.

From my personal experience of walking with Dr. McCartney down the streets of any of the islands of the Bahamas is always the same. We can't go more than approximately 10 feet when someone doesn't run up and say "Dr. McCartney you saved my life (or someone in their family's life)." The two authors are truly living legends.

Drs. McCartney and Neville explain their "Therapeutic Learning Process" and "McNev Process" in terms that can be understood by all. The reader concludes that by reading the book they can improve their own life as well as the lives of their love ones and friends.

—*Drs. Tom and Leslie Tworoger*
Dr. Tom Tworger is a Professor of Entrepreneurship
Dr. Leslie Tworoger is an Associate Professor of Management
Both are at the H. Wayne Huizenga School of
Business and Entrepreneurship, Nova Southeastern University
Fort Lauderdale, Florida

Tim McCartney's personal and professional journey with Mike Neville is truly inspiring in this most interesting read. The dedication, compassion and flexibility they brought to the profession is what made them such a successful team in a most diverse and challenging environment. The concepts and strategies outlined in **U-Turn** provide excellent tools for the layman and a much greater understanding of the human psyche. This book delivers exceptional experiences to a wider audience.

—Jill & Peter Furzer
Retired Tourism and Hotel Executives

———————

Tim McCartney's and Mike Neville's little book *U-Turn* is a readable and fascinating excursion through the often successful attempts of two professionals to engage with the deep social and psychological problems of a small state – the seven hundred island archipelago of the Bahamas. Starting appropriately with their own very different backgrounds (McCartney is Bahamian while Neville is Irish and trained in the UK), the book traces the history of how they came together and worked to combat problems of drug addiction, stress and mental disease, developing along the way their own unique programs based on individual as well as large group interaction. *U-Turn* provides searing insights into the mental health problems faced by small states, but goes far beyond that, to suggest workable solutions for the managing of mental health problems in any jurisdiction in the twenty-first century.

—Brian Meeks, Professor of Social and Political Change
Director, the Sir Arthur Lewis Institute
of Social and Economic Studies
The University of the West Indies

U-Turn is an intriguing book full of personal development concepts and heart-warming stories on how we change, evolve, develop, manage stress, anxiety and depression. It even explores the best means of managing mid-life crisis! The authors emphasize that individuals and organizations must take responsibility for their decisions in order to properly help others and make the world a better place for everyone.

U-Turn emphasizes that success in life, stressful events and change management are matters of choice rather than automatic results of personality or genetics. If you want to know how to become a better manager of your life, read this book to discover practical suggestions for properly resolving the problems and challenges you face each day. The book also helps you better assist others as it is full of great stories on how the authors helped patients in their roles as doctors, psychiatrists and therapists.

Effective management of your life starts by controlling your thoughts. Only with this control can the rest of your life fall into place as envisioned. Everyone has the ability to choose thoughts, feelings, and actions, so choose your responses in any given moment, role model them and spread the message of *U-Turn* to others throughout the world.

—Dr. Bahaudin G. Mujtaba,
Author of ***Coaching and Performance Management***;
Professor of Management at Nova Southeastern University

———————

As usual with books and articles written by Timothy McCartney and Mike Neville, *U-Turn* holds your attention from the beginning to the end. They intersperse serious psychological information with amusing anecdotes.

Their contribution to the psychological welfare of the Bahamas has been invaluable, not only in the daily counseling of their patients but also in seminars, articles and books such as *U-Turn*.

We can all learn something from *U-Turn* and maybe by reading this publication, written by two such gentle and kind men. It will help us all make the *U-Turn* we need.

—Norbert F. Boissiere
Chairman, FamGuard Corporation and
Family Guardian Insurance Company Limited
Nassau, The Bahamas

———————

Thirty-three years ago, I sat, as a student, in a group clinical therapy session conducted by therapists Dr. Tim McCartney and Dr. Mike Neville. I saw positive and effective change take place, at that time, with many participants and this left an indelible memory. The sessions were conducted with humanity, humility, humor, and honesty - the basic tenets on which their book, **U-Turn** is presented by these two extraordinary authors.

U-Turn is a humorous and well-written account, alternating between these two interesting men, describing adventurous upbringings and challenging professional choices and training. The synergy flows between them harmoniously as their mutual support intertwines like a clinical ballet.

In this brilliantly executed guide for students and lay readers, **U-Turn** introduces a new and holistic concept of therapy called the **Therapeutic Learning Process**. This stimulating introspection for self-development, is a *vade mecum* presented with interest and care, as a candid, though refreshing, prescription showing that patients may be healed in due time.

U-Turn is a product of the excitement and brilliance Drs. McCartney and Neville incorporate from each of their disciplines, the healing techniques that were tried, tested and proven over the years, naturally leading to the development of their **Therapeutic Learning Process**.

U-Turn©

Exploring Directions and How To Get There

Timothy McCartney Ph.D.
Mike Neville MBE

Tomorrow's Key
1624 Bonnie Brae Street, No. 6
Houston, Texas 77006

First edition published November 2013

For information about special discounts for bulk purchases or about booking the authors as event speakers, please contact Dr. McCartney at the email address below. Requests for permission to make copies of any part of this work should be emailed to:

Tim: mccartne@nova.edu
Mike: mnevil@batelnet.bs

Designed by Trisha Keel

Manufactured in the United States of America.

1 3 5 7 9 10 8 6 4 2

McCartney, Ph.D., Timothy and Mike Neville MBE
U-Turn : Exploring Directions and How To Get There

ISBN-13: 978-1492238324
ISBN-10: 1492238325

This book is dedicated to our wives,
Pauline and Sandra,
who continue attempting
to keep us focused.

TABLE OF CONTENTS

Acknowledgements   *xiii*

Preface   *xv*

Introduction   *xvii*

Chapter 1: Beginnings   1

Chapter 2: Evolving   10

Chapter 3: Partnerships   23

Chapter 4: Using Your Own Tools   32

Chapter 5: The Therapeutic Learning Process©   39

Chapter 6: Individual Challenges   62

Chapter 7: The McNev Process™   71

Chapter 8: Some Societal Issues   85

Chapter 9: Predictions   107

Bibliography/References   *129*

Author Biographies   *131*

Acknowledgments

My (Tim's) good friend, the late Arthur Hailey (author of *Airport, Hotel, Wheels, The Money Changers,* etc.), once shared with me that *It takes a village to write a book*. He would choose a topic, research it and mobilize his expert resources for two years – then take a year to write it!

We (Tim and Mike) have talked about writing a book of this type for more than twenty years. We have written scientific papers, chapters for books and articles, but never have settled down to write an *eclectic* book. Many times, when we would plan to discuss some structure and content for a book, we would be sabotaged by eating delicious curries cooked by Mike, usually of wild boar that he hunted on Inagua (a Bahamian island), or other times spent sampling gourmet foods and wines in Ft. Lauderdale.

This book would still be only an idea if it were not for the encouragement of Tim's Dean, Dr. J. Preston Jones of the H. Wayne Huizenga School of Business and Entrepreneurship, Nova Southeastern University, in Ft. Lauderdale, Florida. Tim applied for and was awarded a six months sabbatical and the major part of that contract was to *finish* a manuscript for a book.

Tracie Cooper, Faculty Coordinator, played a pivotal role. She not only deciphered Tim's handwriting, but typed the first draft. She coordinated Tim's writing with Mike's as he emailed his drafts to her from the Bahamas. Tracie provided the authors with so many courtesies we are convinced that without her, we would not have completed the book!

We thank Stanley Burnside and Eddie Minnis, Bahamian artists and political cartoonists for their permission to use some of their material depicting Tim and Mike's involvement with the Bahamian community.

We are indebted to persons mentioned on pages and the cover of the book who critiqued, edited, encouraged and were kind enough to write testimonials of their impressions of the content.

We thank Dr. Walter Natemeyer for writing the Preface, suggesting corrections and referring us to our editor/publisher! We really lucked out with Trisha Keel!! Her enthusiasm was infectious. She edited, made suggestions, and returned answers to our questions with *lightening speed* reaction time. She is a professional *par excellence!*

Our comfort and strength comes from our spouses, Pauline and Sandra. They have put up with us for a long time – two adult professionals, more fun-loving than serious, who are actually *teenagers* at heart! Thanks for being there for us.

We are blessed to have caring, loving children, grands and great grands. Our relationships and time spent with them makes all of our lives blessed and worthwhile.

Tim McCartney and *Mike Neville*

PREFACE

A couple of years ago, my esteemed colleague and best friend
Dr. Paul Hersey invited me to team-teach a Leadership Capstone
Course in the MBA Program at Nova Southeastern University.

During that week, I met several Nova School of Business
faculty members and their spouses. Among them were Dr. Tim
McCartney and his wife Pauline. "Doc" Hersey and his wife Suzie
had told me many stories about Dr. Tim's amazing success as a
clinical psychologist in the Bahamas.

During that Leadership Capstone Course, and the same course a
year later, I had the opportunity to get to know, love and respect
Tim and Pauline McCartney. As Doc and Suzie Hersey had told
me, they were extraordinary people whose brilliance, love of life
and kindness always captivated everyone around them.

I felt very honored when Tim asked me to review the book that he
had written with his long-time business partner, Dr. Mike Neville.
Reading *U-Turn*© was a wonderful adventure for me. It gave
me great insight into the challenges, responsibilities and joys of
counseling people struggling with their journey through life.

U-Turn© – *Exploring Directions and How to Get There* captivated me
with its in-depth description of the authors' ancestral African and
European roots, their fascinating international educational odyssey,
their serendipitous rendezvous in the Bahamas, and their evolution
as a highly successful psycho-psychiatric partnership.

Tim and Mike weave their personal stories into a strong fabric of
psychoanalytic approaches and fascinating experiences which serve
as the basis for their Therapeutic Learning Process© (TLP).

Tim and Mike provide a systematic review of their McNev
Process™ and methodology. They also provide a thought-
provoking overview of the challenges individuals and societies face

as they wrestle with the many problems they encounter in their journey through life.

A consistent theme runs through this book. As individuals, organizations or societies, we are responsible for our decisions. We always have choices. *U-Turn©* teaches us how to take control of our own thoughts and feelings, encourages us to make wise decisions, and helps us to choose to celebrate the joy of life. Enjoy this book and remember: *Every Day Is a Gift!*

Walter E. Natemeyer, Ph.D.
Chairman and CEO
North American Training and Development, Inc.

INTRODUCTION

We (Tim McCartney and Mike Neville) have been talking about this book for more than ten years! We have written manuscripts, developed highly structured textbook styles, and experimented with novel-like formats, but for some reason, never felt comfortable with our efforts. We have collected and kept what we have written, but it was only recently when Mike paid a visit to Fort Lauderdale that we found out that our thinking was finally in sync.

"Why not write in the style in which we conduct our seminars and workshops? Why not share our experiences with our patients and clients, and proffer our insights regarding organizations and the workplace. Let's just write, share ourselves and simply let it flow." Mike suggested strongly – but not so strongly – this has happened many times before, but McCartney was thinking the same thing!!

In the past, we have often started to conduct a workshop and after five minutes, realized, without saying a word, that our pre-structured presentation guidelines were just not appropriate. Mike or I would then change into a mode or style that immediately gave us the feedback that we anticipated and successfully allowed us to achieve positive goals, at that particular time and place.

This book is not a textbook, it is not a novel, and surely not poetry, but somewhat autobiographical in that we have shared what we believe honestly, without being politically correct (which has never been our style). We have attempted to relate personal and professional experiences that, at most times, have worked very well. This book is a sharing book! We have never taken ourselves too seriously, and perhaps our shared genetic Irish backgrounds have blessed us with the gift of gab, an enjoyment of life and a *joie-de-vivre* that we have experienced with our families, friends and yes – clients.

We share a unique relationship, as unique and creative persons from very different ethno-psycho-social backgrounds. Even our physical selves have earned us the description of "Mutt and Jeff." Mike Neville is a medical doctor specializing in psychiatry.

Tim McCartney is a Clinical Psychologist and the Paul Hersey Chair in Leadership and Organizational Behavior and Professor of Management at the H. Wayne Huizenga School of Business and Entrepreneurship, Nova Southeastern University in Fort Lauderdale, Florida.

McCartney and Neville Consulting Associates has worked as an Organizational Development Consulting firm, with many national and multi-national companies worldwide.

At the beginning of our individual and collective practices, the many ethno-cultural, trans-national and idiosyncratic situations we encountered had not been described or experienced in our formal educational training in the USA, Switzerland, France, Ireland and England.

We began our formal practice in Nassau, the capital of the Bahamas. We were thrust into a complex culture that had recently undergone a quiet revolution when the power and socio-economic structure began to change from the old politico-social order of an oligarchic regime of a few wealthy white men (some with a "touch of the brush") who practiced discrimination and social distance even though the majority of Bahamians were black.

This diverse culture consisted of everything from the rich and famous of Lyford Cay and the Eastern road, to small communities of lower middle class and poor people, primarily from over-the-hill pockets of African and mixed ancestry, to expatriates from many other countries. This transition of power and *new* social order demanded the need for investigation, trial and error exploration, creativity and grit.

We had to deal with a wide variety of experiences, including:

a. A banker from New York on a three year contract, referred by his psychoanalyst for continuing sessions in the Bahamas.

b. A female Canadian accountant, married to a Bahamian, with serious phobias especially the fear of cockroaches.

c. Wives from various ethnic groups (Greek, Indian, Syrian, etc.) who were actually beaten and/or severely abused by their husbands who believed it was their *cultural right* to do so when they got out of line.

d. Adolescent children, primarily of Caribbean expatriates, illegal immigrants and some Bahamians, who were *falling out* (collapsing) with epileptic-form symptoms for no apparent medical reasons.

e. Employees from many business firms who were threatening to strike or even engage in violence because their recently appointed black manager was *petty, revengeful, not trained* and was *unfair* to them, unlike their former *white* (expatriate) manager who was kind to them.

f. Many persons who were presenting with interesting but strange behavior believing that someone had *fixed* them or put a *hex* (magic spell) on them. Many had already consulted *obeah* (a sort of Caribbean sorcery) men or women and had engaged in interesting cures.

g. The usual mental and psychological syndromes of depression, schizophrenia, addictions, personality disorders, marital and interpersonal problems with cultural twists.

Our educational background gave us the basic, traditional tools in trying to cope with these unique problems, but for some reason, except for more obvious conditions and prescription/medical interventions, we were bothered when we were not successful in providing for our clients sustained and/or acceptable coping skills. We expected our patients/clients to understand their real condition and to slowly replace their lifestyles with effective decision-making processes that motivated them, allowed for dealing with failures, and helped them to find balance in their lives that would provide a modicum of security and well-being.

We began to realize that this population expected us to be direction-oriented professionals who reinforced authority figures, prescribed *medicines*, auscultated them and told them what to do! They wanted clear guidelines as to what we thought was right or wrong, good or bad and an inter-active doctor, sensitive to their religions, folklore and superstition belief systems, especially since they were paying us for this advice!!

When we started our Organization Development Consultations, we followed acceptable processes that were taught in Business Schools and unfortunately succumbed to some of the fads of personality questionnaires, managerial grids, leadership methodologies and other approaches that appeared to be too "culture-bound."
The fact that we were sufficiently flexible to resort to simplistic fundamentals and adapting a language that anyone would understand and apply, gave positive results with national and multi-national organizations. McCartney and Neville Consulting Associates made a bold decision to provide a basic structure in fundamental constructs, use research, consultant realities and best practices as to develop a holistic, transcultural and more practical paradigm.

Our Therapeutic Learning Process© (TLP) was eventually conceived, developed and refined. It became the principal guideline for our culturally unbiased methodology extracted from existing theories and more easily adaptable methodologies and notions about human behavior.

TLP has grown, through trial and error to be a successful and strategically planned process that allows for individuals and groups to learn about themselves and apply what they have learned. They can easily identify, understand and implement the languages and concepts that are explained. The professional provides appropriate and realistic alternatives for the client to consider, specify the positive and negative consequences of their choices, and encourages them to learn from their mistakes. They slowly begin to build self-esteem, self-reliance and security from their own experiences, realizing that failure (as a fallible human being) is one of the experiences that give them insights into a balanced, healthy life.

The title of the book happened by an incident one weekend. McCartney was laboring to find a title by looking at some of the written content, and developing references. He became very frustrated and started tearing up paper, making unintelligible noises and just being miserable!

One of his grandsons, Daniel Forrest, was visiting. After a while, Daniel wanted to find out why *Papa* was so frustrated and not paying any attention to him. He had never seen his Papa like this and was a bit annoyed that Papa had not found time to take him to McDonald's for a kid's meal and strawberry milkshake.

Papa explained to Daniel that he was writing a book with Dr. Neville and they needed a title for the book. Daniel, whose father was a brilliant physician, knew that his Papa and Dr. Neville were the kind of doctors who helped people who had *meltdowns* and took drugs.

Daniel, who is very smart and a creative artist, suddenly exclaimed "Papa, I got it!" He was quiet for a moment and then said, "Give me your pen and I'll show you what you should do!"

He then drew two U-Turn road signs and said that we should name the book *U-Turn*. "You and Dr. Neville are always giving people advice. They can either follow the right sign or turn where they should not turn and get into trouble.

"Brilliant!" I thought.

I immediately telephoned Mike in the Bahamas and related what had just happened.

"That *is* brilliant!" he said. "This is *exactly* what we have been looking for."

We now had a title, but we needed to explain on the cover of the book, what *U-Turn* was all about.

A few months after this incident, Dr. Paul Hersey was visiting Nova. He and Ken Blanchard developed *Situational Leadership* which is cited in all of the Organizational Behavior courses and textbooks. Ken Blanchard subsequently wrote *The One Minute Manager* and developed a very successful consulting company. Paul Hersey continued his research and the development of *Situational Leadership*.

His Center for Leadership Studies has trained over ten million people throughout the world. "Doc" Hersey was also a Distinguished Visiting Professor at Nova Southeastern University in Fort Lauderdale, established training scholarships and donated the impressive statue that is found in the atrium of the Wayne Huizenga School of Business and Entrepreneurship. He also established the first endowed Chair in *Leadership and Organizational Behavior,* which one of these authors, Tim McCartney, currently holds.

Tim shared the conceptualization of this book with Dr. Hersey and showed him some of the manuscript that had been written. He was fascinated by the title of this book and gave us the explanation of *U-Turn© - Determining the Real Directions and How to Get There.* He also agreed to write the Preface to the book.

Regrettably, Doc passed away in December of 2012. This is not only a great loss of a mentor and friend to McCartney, but also to Nova Southeastern University and the world! Doc was a brilliant academician and a person of incredible charity and integrity. He will be missed!

U-Turn© is based on more than eighty years combined personal and professional experiences of the authors. We have used a free-flowing writing style, shifting sometimes without warning from the philosophy of Mike to the anecdotal stories of Tim. The brilliant lyrical prose of Mike and the more basic simplistic text – and sometimes wordy ideas of McCartney should provide for interesting reading.

We sincerely hope that this book will be a joy to read, be informative and educational, and provide a positive impact on our readers.

U-Turn!!

Tim McCartney
Mike Neville

U-Turn©

U-Turn©

Exploring Directions and How To Get There

U-Turn©

Chapter 1

BEGINNINGS

May your mornings bring joy
and your evenings bring peace.

Every problem is unique...

I have never fully understood why we talk of our stomachs grumbling or growling. Mine (Mike) is much more cunning and devious. It sends colorful pictures of gorgeous, exciting foods straight to my consciousness, and right then, I was working on images of some conch salad with limes, goat peppers, and maybe a crisp fresh French baguette.

"Doc, there is someone to see you."

My reverie was broken. My secretary was at the door and my thoughts of lunch gone.

"I am not expecting anyone. Does he have an appointment?"

"No," she said, "but apparently he is threatening to kill himself."

"OK, OK. Send him in."

A strong heavily built young man walked into my office. He looked sad and downcast and slowly slumped into a chair. He did not say anything, just gazed down at the floor.

I asked, "How can I help?" No response!

"I gather that you feel life just isn't worth living," I said.

He looked up, with large sad eyes, tears welling up at the sides.

"She left me," he said.

Life is full of these human tragedies. Relationships can unleash many emotions – jealousy, rage, depression – and this can sometimes lead to murder or suicide. Our emergency rooms and crime statistics are replete with anecdotes of domestic violence, so these matters must be taken seriously. Perhaps, I thought, if we talked about his ex-girlfriend, I could find a way to get him to realize that his setback was not the end of the world and there would be other girls and new relationships.

"What was about her that you most liked? What was it that made you fall in love with her?" I asked.

I was expecting him to talk of her beauty, her stunning body, her eyes or perhaps her intelligence or scintillating wit.

His eyes spilled over, the tears flowed and he looked into my eyes searching for understanding.

"It was her hairy legs."

―――――

In another part of the hospital Dr. McCartney sat in his office.

"Hello, Dr. McCartney here"

"Hi Tim, John Spencer. How are you? I have a patient that I would like for you to see."

"Great! It's good to finally get started. I've been frustrated these last three weeks without an office, psychological instruments or even starting to see patients on an individual basis. I have enjoyed though, our morning rounds on the wards with the team and am happy with the leadership role that you project so well."

"Thanks! It's good to have you back and we desperately need your expertise! Anyhow, I have a very interesting lady whom I would like for you to see. She was admitted to the ward two weeks ago, but you have not met her because we have had to heavily medicate her to bring her to some state where we can at least interview her. She demonstrates a diagnostic difficulty because there are so many factors that mimic various dysfunctional states. We're puzzled and are hoping that you might be able to help. Believe me, you will find her very interesting. I will send her complete notes with the attendant who will bring her to see you whenever you can."

"Okay, John. Actually, I have an opening in an hour. I'm just putting the finishing touches on this office, which is small but quite comfortable. I'm also glad that Administration has provided a couch and a very nice comfortable chair for me. It makes for a welcoming environment. Your referral will be my first in the Bahamas and I look forward to seeing her. I will probably need two to three sessions to complete my observations and testing. Perhaps a day afterward, I could get a report to you. Of course, it would depend on my work load and it will be interesting to see how many referrals I begin to have. I just wonder whether people and the professionals know what I'm about."

"Tim, trust me. I have enough patients to keep you busy for at least a year. Once people see your positive impact on our mental health program, I think you are in for an interesting time my friend."

"Thanks – I'll get back to you, as soon as I can."

Within the hour, a young lady with wild looking shifty eyes entered my office with an male attendant from the female ward, who gave me a rather large file.

"Do you want me to sit and wait here with her, Dr. McCartney?"

"No, I prefer that you wait outside. I can always call if I need you."

The young lady, 29 years old, attractive and neatly dressed, looked at me suspiciously and kept standing.

"Hello. I'm Doctor McCartney. Your doctor has asked me to give you a few tests so that he can better understand your condition in order to help you get better. Would you please sit down over here?"

The lady looked at me, and she looked around the room. She started a short gallop towards the chair; then circled the chair and raised herself up with her hand in front of her – "Heehee! Heehee!" – neighing like a horse. Then, in a crouching position, she started galloping and neighing around my office.

"Ride me, doctor! Ride me, doctor!" she said, getting louder and louder. "Heehee! Heehee! Heehee!"

"Okay, I'll ride you later, but could you just have a seat for a moment? I want to find out a bit about you first, and then I guess, I can go for a ride."

She sat down on the floor abruptly, got on her back, lifted up her legs and slowly lowered them, closed her eyes and started to sob very quietly. I allowed her to continue without disturbing her for a while, then she stopped sobbing and slowly opened her eyes.

"Are you ready for me to ask you a few questions?" I asked.

"No! I'm sleepy. I want to sleep. I'm tired! I'm tired! I'm tired," she kept repeating.

I took her by her hands and slowly helped her off the floor. I asked her to sit in the chair.

"You sure you don't want to talk to me?"

"No, not today – another time, another time, another time."

She then slumped in the chair, closed her eyes and appeared to be going to sleep.

I'm going to send you back to your room, where you can sleep more comfortably. I will come to see you tomorrow and if you want to, we can talk."

I called for the attendant, and shared with him what had happened. He just smiled and said, "I thought she had gotten over the horse thing, but I guess she still needs more treatment and time."

I telephoned John and explained what had happened.

"I told you that she was interesting!"

"I don't know what's really going on, John, but I will visit her on a daily basis on the ward to observe her behavior. When she's ready for testing, I'll do it. You should continue to medicate her, and I think she will soon be sufficiently calm to be psychologically evaluated."

———

Whew!! What the hell am I in for? My first patient in the Bahamas is really psychotic, and decompensating big time into believing that she is a horse?

———

One of the many wonders of mental health is the lack of walls, unless, of course, we put them there ourselves. There can be all kinds of different places that a consultation can take place; the beach, the park, the bar, just about anywhere!

One of the most extreme differences is the switch from Fox Hill Prison to Lyford Cay. The prison, which the media have dubbed "Fox Hell Prison," is the government-run lock-up for the whole Bahamas. It houses some very interesting characters!

"Any particular reason why you killed all those taxi drivers?" I asked.

"It began by accident. We were robbing an armored vehicle and the getaway car would not start; so we jumped into a hacker's (an unlicensed taxi driver) car and made him drive off at gunpoint. When we were well away and felt that we had gotten away, the driver just really pissed me off. So I shot him".

"OK…but why kill the others? You killed about nine taxi drivers altogether over a short period of time, from what I have been told."

"Well that's the point isn't it? It felt so good, better than drugs or sex. I just felt so powerful, I just had to do it again and it just became part of all our robberies."

I already had a feeling that this man had no conscience, no guilt, no remorse, but you still ask the questions, right?

"Do you feel bad about any of this?"

"Yes"

In my mind I thought, well, at least he has the decency to try to lie.

"Yes, I do," he said. "I had always planned to kill one hundred people before I was caught!"

The prison has no toilets. The cells have buckets that get emptied each day. The hot humid Caribbean weather creates smells and droves of flies that are hard to put into words.

———

It is afternoon at Lyford Cay, a beautiful gated community, home of the rich and famous, at the western end of New Providence as far from the prison as is possible on this small island, but even further in terms of how life seems.

At Lyford Cay, the toilets are not even referred to in such base terms. They glitter with gold and steel, surrounded by the best marble that money can buy. Enticing colors of black, white, and azure; all sorts of beauty where one can sit in the cool air conditioned space and ponder. This is so different from the Fox Hill prisoner's bucket which he shares with four or five other tragic figures in a sweltering concrete cubicle with fetid air, awful stenches and nothing resembling hope.

That afternoon I was not there to wax lyrically about the philosophical unfairness of the world. I was there to see an elderly lady who had cut her wrists the night before. I had been told that she was very wealthy. Actually, that was not news to me since it was an enclave where the millionaires feel insecure with the billionaires and the billionaires cringe when talking about the trillionaires, but she was rich! The woman was in her mid-seventies and lived with a younger boyfriend.

The house was fabulous. I was escorted by a uniformed housekeeper to the master bedroom. The floor white marble, the bed, mushroomed white silk, and to my surprise, the ceiling and back of the bed were covered with ornate mirrors.

The dear lady propped up in bed was both diminutive and desolate. She tearfully told me that her boyfriend was drinking too much and she could no longer bear to live. Her depression was so severe it was infectious. It was almost a relief to go out to the kitchen to talk to the boyfriend about his drinking. That certainly seemed an easy enough problem to resolve. The boyfriend, though allegedly younger, did not look it. He had had a long career on the stage but frankly looked more as if he had been hit by the stage.

He told me in a raspy quivering tone that he had throat cancer. His voice box had been cut out and he communicated through a "Darth Vader" contraption that sounded straight out of Star Wars! Did he drink? Certainly! He had a penchant for an aged Remy Martin that he poured down his feeding tube!

––––––––––

All these problems have solutions, not necessarily cures, and not always good solutions, but solutions none the less. Rarely are they instantaneous. Rather they have a slow evolution as choices become clearer and as options are tried then reinforced or discarded, depending on their success.

Even in these vignettes the opportunities for a *U-Turn* are varied. The two suicidal clients were treated with antidepressant medication and talking therapy to restore their self esteem and both did very well. The lady with the delusions about the horse was treated with antipsychotic medication and talking therapy to to give insight into her delusions remained on medication and was able to live out of hospital with limitations on her life. Our friend with the feeding tube chose not to stop drinking and eventually died whereas after a complex trial the serial killer remains in prison.

We have both worked with so many individuals over the years that it is hard to keep track of them all. To say we have a varied experience of life and its problems would be putting it mildly. It was thereby a natural progression for us to work together, not just on interesting individual cases. but to jump at the chance to go into organizations and deal with problems on a much larger scale.

We were first asked to help the major firms in Grand Bahama to deal with the cocaine epidemic of the early eighties. The Bahamas had not had a long history of major drug abuse, and cocaine quite frankly, caught the country by surprise. It was called *freebase* back then, now is known as **crack**. The speed and power of the epidemic was so awful that it seemed as if the drug lords had used the Bahamas as a huge laboratory to see just how addictive and how profitable this scourge could be. We were asked to help the industrial complexes in Grand Bahama deal with the absenteeism, the increased accident rates and the frightening human costs that were attacking the moral fiber of the nation.

Chapter 2

EVOLVING

Beautiful young people are acts of nature.
Beautiful old people are works of art.

Understanding our roots can develop professionalism...

Who or what gives us the right to jump into other people's problems, crisis and chaos?

Simply put: no one. We try to use our training, our belief systems, in fact, our very selves to help others. We have no right. We just try to do our best.

Why should you read or listen to what we have to say?

Good question!

What makes us who and what we are?

Psychology 101 would suggest that it is a combination of our genetics and our environment. Most textbooks leave it there, missing the importance of choice. The fact simply put is that no matter what cards we are dealt, we have some control over our destiny.

We too are the product of our genetic code (what we inherited from our forebears), our culture, our life's experiences and indeed our training and then the choices that we have made as we have travelled through life. Let us digress and share some of the bits and pieces that have helped to develop us.

I (Mike) was born in Manchester, England in 1948, and my early memories are basically very happy. We lived comfortably, though unlike now, I was blissfully unaware of what we did not have. Communications were still in their infancy and so it was easy to be happy with what you had or did not have. Now it is so much harder because of the daily bombardments from TV and the internet reminding everyone of what they should have. My parents were both Irish, both from Cork and both physicians. It was a part of my growth to hear the family tales. How true? Who knows, but still a part of growing.

My dad came from a farm on the river a few miles from Macroom, County Cork. The farm was called Ballytrasna. We spent summers in a seaside town called Youghal – a town with a colorful past. It was home to monasteries guarded by the Knights Templar and the house where Sir Walter Raleigh had lived. It was a place of fond memories for me, such as the small "unsinkable" clinker-built wooden boat that the local police sergeant built for us at Dad's request. It was a small boat that lived up to its billing: it did not sink!

There was also the annual pilgrimage to Bealnablath, where General Michael Collins was assassinated on August 22, 1922. My father died before I was old enough to ask him about it, but it must have been devastating for him as the killing took place so close to the farm while he was away at medical school. He had been elected Captain of Kilmurray Company, which consisted of men from the old Dooniskey Company, the national volunteers in Kilmurray, and men from Bealnablath. He was arrested after the Easter Rising in 1916. The leaders in Dublin were shot and many men were sent to England to internment camps. Dad was held in the Bridewell jail in Cork, unsure of his fate. He was allowed a visit by two of his sisters, who told me that he asked for a blanket as he was cold, a Bible as he expected to be executed, and finally, his Latin book – in case he survived he still wanted to go to medical school. He was lucky he was held by the regular army and his young age led to a release.

He went on to medical school, played rugby for Munster and eventually moved to Manchester in the north of England. He volunteered for the British army in the Second World War and one of his treasured possessions was a silver cigarette case given to him by the very same battalion that held him prisoner years before!

My mother was also a medical doctor who played camogie for Cork University. She was wonderful, and stood by our family no matter what. One of my cousins later told me that after his father died, she asked my mother how she managed with three robust sons rebelling against society. She said "Oh, you just hang in there." What wonderful advice!

All was not however as idyllic as it might have been. After we moved to England in the area in north Manchester where we lived, we got attached to a group of kids called the Grant Street gang and much of our time was spend preparing for fights with the Middlesex Road gang. I am not sure how we got into it, but I was younger than anyone else, and things happen.

The battlers involved the use of catapults made with wooden centerpieces from trees and o-rings *borrowed* from a car repair shop. That all came to an early end one day when it was raining heavily. We took refuge in an abandoned air raid shelter where we started a fire. I do not believe we meant any harm but, after visits from the police, the family priest was called for some sort of summit meeting and before long, it was off to Ditcham Park, a prep school run by Benedictine monks. I still remember the awful loneliness of being left in the middle of nowhere with these strange men in total control of my destiny.

There were some good memories though. I liked the sports and exploring the countryside, but I was constantly in trouble. The priests and I started a battle for control that would last for the rest

of my school days. I did not call it control back then. They had
all kinds of rules, I broke them, and, if I was caught I was caned.
The only thing this type of punishment taught me was to avoid
being caught. Not that that helped; I would then be caned for some
irrelevent minor offence!

I certainly learned a lot in childhood. Life was usually not fair but
I could still retain some control over my destiny. I was determined
to never let the priests defeat my rebellion, although it was certainly
tough at times. It was years later that I understood that the school
was attempting to create administrators for a colonial service that
no longer existed and it all had little to do with me.

My father's death from lung cancer made the rebellion more
intense, but at least I decided that it would be a smart move not to
smoke! Even more valuable was the lesson from his life that there is
no reason to be stuck in one line of thought. At one stage, fighting
the English seemed appropriate, then later it seemed equally
appropriate to fight for them.

I sometimes wonder if the losses and the brutality of boarding
school life left me depressed, as my next move was a gap year when
I hitchhiked all over Europe by myself. I was either very brave or
did not care if I lived or died. I know that I see many youngsters
like that in my practice these days. "If God wants me, He can have
me" is the kind of thinking that opens up so many risks.

I went to Medical school at the Royal College of Surgeons in
Dublin, Ireland. After all, I had grown up thinking I was Irish
and had suffered the difficulties of being part of the minority
in boarding school. I was quickly put to rights. I had an English
accent so I was English – whether I liked it or not.

I enjoyed med school immensely. Life revolved around rugby and
a pub called the Toby Jug. Medicine was an afterthought, perhaps
best illustrated by an oral exam in anatomy conducted around a
cadaver. The question was particularly obtuse and when it became

apparent that only I knew the answer, our professor smiled.

"Neville," said the professor. "Ah, Neville. You remind me of a patient with a head injury – and even they have occasional lucid periods."

I was in Paris as captain of the combined Dublin hospitals rugby team when the awful killings took place in Derry. The tragedy became known as "Bloody Sunday." The team was nearly all Irish, but the plane was a British Caledonian charter so we were banned from returning to Dublin. No money, a rugby team stuck at an airport: a recipe for disaster. One of the more enterprising fellows discovered the number to dial to get onto the public address system:

"Will Fergus Donnelly please go to the Place Pigalle where the largest, smelliest whore in the whole of Paris is waiting for him?" boomed out over the tannoy (public address) system. Things rapidly went from bad to worse as the number changed hands and the messages became more outrageous. Meanwhile another entrepreneur was organizing a nose picking contest in the first class lounge. I was able to negotiate free beer and some food as long as I could keep the lads in this small bar well away from the regular passengers until they could get us back to Ireland.

Eventually we flew to Shannon airport and landed without air traffic control help. We were bused to Dublin where we found out that the few "English lads had been told not to come to college in case there was trouble." A week off never went astray, but when we heard that the IRA was going to burn down the English Embassy it was too big to miss. We put on our best Irish accents and off to Merrion Square with everyone else to see if they could do it!

At the appointed time a covered truck drove slowly into the square and stopped in front of the Embassy. The covers came off and the *lads* were there with a mortar aimed at the buildings.

"You have two minutes to get out of the way," said a fellar (fellow) with a loud hailer. The Gardai looked at each other and ran.

The explosions seemed huge and the whole building caught fire to loud cheers from the crowd. The next week back in college one of my Irish colleagues said to me, "We showed you, you f_ckers." I did not have the energy to explain my heritage or that the Dublin tax payers would be stuck with the bill. I had had a great week off and was beginning to get confused about all this English-Irish stuff anyway. Graduation was a sad day. We all wondered why we had *not* failed.

———————

The specter of a life of responsibility was overwhelming in the space of an exam result. We had gone from irresponsible gombines (jerks) to doctors who needed to be pillars of the community, a jump that not all of my friends were able to make!

It was off to the Bahamas to do my internship. It sounded like an exotic place, and little did I know that it would eventually become my home.

The first glimpse of a career in mental health occurred when I was doing obstetrics and gynecology. An attractive young girl had been admitted the night before. She was wearing a surgical gown tied at the front when she suddenly took off racing out of the ward and out into the car park.

"Catch her!" shouted someone, and, like an idiot I took off after her. She raced along the side of the building, the gown billowing behind her like a cape, with me in hot pursuit of this naked patient.

"Two to one on the white doctor!" cried a painter half way up the building on some scaffolding.

I never chased another patient and never will!

I met my wife on the same ward. She was the nurse in charge of the newborn nursery. I don't know if she was impressed with my running, but shortly after that, I broke my leg playing rugby, so running stopped for a while.

Sandra has traced her roots back to the Yoruba people from West Africa. She has been my soul mate ever since we met, calming some of the storms in my head and always helping me to see the more rational and more accepted approaches to problems. I still have trouble listening, but after thirty-five years of married life together, we must have gotten something right.

We went back to Manchester together so that we could both further our education. For a while I worked for my mother's general practice. I realized that this was not for me when, one sunny summer morning, I was in the surgery and an elderly lady came in for a consultation. I felt she was on too much medication and painstakingly explained it all to her. She left seemingly happy but met another old dear just outside my open window.

"Which doctor is on this morning?" The new lady asked.

"It's the young Dr. Neville" she said.

"What's he like? She asked.

"Ooh," she said, "He is nice, but don't know much yet."

———————

There was a job in Psychiatry in the local hospital and I thought that I really knew very little about Psychiatry, so a six month rotation seemed like a good experience. Well, I never left. I had found my niche, so psychiatry was about to become my life's work.

One of my aunts had been one of the first female medical graduates from Cork University and did not think very highly of psychiatry. I went to tell her that I was going to do Psychiatry and she made a face. I said "Go on and say what you have got to say. I know you are not too pleased."

She looked right at me and said, "You will go crazy, you know." "They all do."

My wife giggled.

"You need not laugh," she said. "The wives go crazy too."

———

We came back to the Bahamas with an enthusiastic naiveté to tackle problems and improve society. I started work at Sandilands, the government mental hospital, and fairly soon I was visited in my office by a giant of a man, whom I came to know as Tim.

"The staff here all thinks you are racist, you know," he said!

———

Hold it!! I'm afraid that I'm jumping the gun. Perhaps it may be useful to give a brief history of Tim's socio-psychological background that eventually brought him to this point in this life.

———

It was December, 1967, and Tim was the first Bahamian with a doctorate in Clinical Psychology working for the Ministry of Health at the only mental health facility in the Bahamas: the Sandilords Rehabilitation Center. This hospital was situated in the quaint village of Fox Hill, adjacent to Her Majesty's Prison in Nassau, Bahamas.

Tim was born in Nassau in 1933, the oldest of eight children, to parents who were born on the Island of Eleuthera and had migrated to Nassau. His father was from Tarpum Bay, a settlement of mixed population, and his mother was from Savannah Sound, just four miles east of Tarpum Bay.

Tim's parents were of mixed heritage. His great grandfather was Freeman McCartney, an Irish seaman from Bilarney, County Cork. He *jumped ship* as his vessel left Tarpum Bay for England, after it was repaired.

Freeman was a *jack of all trades,* and that was passed over to his son, my grandfather, William "McGee" McCartney. Freeman McCartney subsequently fell in love with an African woman – "Aunt Lighty" – of the Fulani tribe from northwestern Nigeria.

She and her father were captured by slave merchants and placed on a boat to the New World. It was intercepted by the British Navy who set them free as they landed in Bermuda. They soon boarded a ship for the Caribbean, but landed in Nassau. Shortly afterwards, they were told that life was better in Eleuthera and they migrated to Tarpum Bay. Her father became a farmer and she did dressmaking. My paternal grandmother (Mae Dorn McCartney) described Aunt Lighty as a tall, dark-skinned, high check-boned woman of incredible beauty.

Freeman found her irresistible! They lived together for a while, but when he became a born-again Christian, he married her a year before the abolition of slavery.

My mother, Cora, of Savannah Sound, was the youngest child of Richard Culmer, a first generation Englishman, who was married to a Clarke who died when my mother was just four or five years old. He subsequently married a Gibson, who was a school teacher and whom I knew very well. My parents were married in Savannah Sound. One week later they moved to Nassau where my father had already bought a home on a hill in Fort Fincastle. It also had an entrance from Mason's Addition down the hill. I was born there and when I was four years old, my father bought another home in another neighborhood which was then called *Bethel's Addition*. It was a quiet neighborhood.

Just below the hill from Government House and the St. Agnes Anglican Church pastor's residence. Our home's back yard was adjacent to a huge property that belonged to the Anglican Diocese and where the Anglican priest had a beautiful two-story home on the top of the hill. Canon George Pyfrom was the pastor of St. Agnes Church, and lived there.

Bethel's Addition was a mixed environment consisting of English, Bahamian, white, black and mixed who subsequently became some of the socio-politico-intellectual *movers* of the Bahamas. The McPhersons, Thompsons, McCartneys, Coopers, Grants, Braces, Keys, Foxes and Culmers were all well-known families of achievers. As Mackey Williams wrote in his book about McPherson Street, "It was a time when neighbors were neighborly, when gentlemen wore hats, when a young boy helped an old lady carry her groceries, when young women were ladies, when children respected their elders, when children were disciplined by parents and neighbors, when laughter was everywhere, and finally, when parents took their children to church on Sundays."

Mackey's grandfather, S.C. McPherson, was an elegant black man, soft-spoken, with a powerful presence and community commitment. He became a Member of Parliament in 1923 for the Southern District and was responsible for saving the Government High School from closing. He organized an Elks Lodge. He was a tailor by profession.

My family grew to provide me with seven siblings: Richard, Cora Mae, William (Wilmac), Joan, Mavis, Clinton and Ann. Our parents always planned something for us to do during the summer vacation. We either visited Eleuthera for a few weeks, or visited my mother's only sister Edith, who lived in Coconut Grove, Florida, or there were occasional visits to New York where I had two uncles and a lot of cousins from my paternal and maternal sides.

I knew from an early age that after high school in the Bahamas, I would go abroad to further my education. My father, who did not have the opportunity to do so, always told me that he wanted to be a doctor (physician), but since he could not go to college, his oldest son had to become a doctor.

In those days, the professions that the majority Bahamians aspired to were medicine, pharmacy, law, religion and becoming a top civil servant. Other areas, (banking, accounting, architecture, etc.) were restricted to either white or very fair-skinned Bahamians.

After graduating from St. John's College (high school) in Nassau, I worked as an apprentice Pharmacist at the Bahamas General Hospital Dispensary (now the Princess Margaret Hospital). My work was so impressive that the Superintendent to the Health Ministry offered me a scholarship to attend the Harriott Watt College in Scotland since there was, at that time, no one with a university degree in Pharmacy. I began to make my plans.

My father was friendly with Reverend Frederick Frey, the Prior of St. Augustine Monastery and Headmaster of a new high school, St. Augustine College, and shared my plans with him. Rev. Frey suggested to my father that I get a general undergraduate degree in America. He also recommended that I attend a small college, St. John's University in Minnesota, his home state. St. John's had a few notable Bahamian graduates including Etienne and Eugene Dupuch. Other Bahamians, Charles Coakley and Jimmy Thompson, were studying there for the priesthood.

My father shared this with me, and I agreed that this was an excellent idea. I used to see movies about the exciting American college life, with its proms, football games, beer busts and parties. I would fantasize about attending a college there. I informed superintendent Knowles of my change of plans and I sent my application to St. John's via Fr. Frey. I was accepted to start in the fall of 1953. The summer of 1953, accompanied by Charles Coakley, Roy Fong Ben and Andrew Curry, I travelled from Miami in a segregated train up to the Mason Dixie Line. We changed trains in Chicago, and then rode on to Minnesota.

It was a wonderful first-ride-in-a-train for me, though I had been on the New York subway and watched trains when I visited Miami. My father and I collected toy trains and liked to hear the bell ring and the whistle blow. We couldn't eat in the dining room on the train, so my Miami relatives fixed lots of fried chicken, potato salad, sandwiches, juice and sodas, which I shared and we all enjoyed.

––––––––

College life at St. John's brought a significant turning point in my life in terms of my two different cultures and values. St. John's was a beautiful environment. It was surrounded by two large lakes, pine trees, fruit trees, cattle, and, at that time, was totally self-supporting. The monks grew their own vegetables, slaughtered pigs and cows, had chickens, and hunted for pheasant. They smoked their bacon and ham, made sauerkraut and baked the most tasteful bread (*Johnny Bread*) that I had ever had.

I was not, at the time, a Roman Catholic, but students had to attend daily Mass, twice yearly retreats, and take a mandatory course in philosophy, ethics or metaphysics. I made lifelong friends, spent holidays with my friends and their families. I learned how to water ski, sang in the St. John's Men's Choir which travelled throughout the mid-western states, took part in an opera (*Die Fledermaus*).

I became a member of the *Moonmisters* dance band, was co-producer of two home coming shows, was co-disc jockey of the first Jazz show with the late Tom Gits. The producer of that show was former congressman, the Honorable Dave Durenberger of Minnesota. I also formed the *Junkanoos*, a Calypso quartet with the late Eddie "Apple" Elliot, (Bahamas) Cyril Paul and Al Fernandez (Trinidad and Venezuela.)

During the summer vacation, we played at some of the hot spots in Minnesota and declined an offer to play in Las Vegas. Cyril Paul and I also appeared on television in Minneapolis with anthropologist, Sister Inez Helger, from the College of St. Benedicts, talking about Caribbean Culture and demonstrating the many instruments used in calypso, the cha-cha, and other music from the region.

———————

It was also, in my senior year, that I fell in love for the first time and got engaged. We never married, however, because I went to Europe to continue my education and she entered the convent to become a nun. While waiting to get into medical school, I was fascinated by psychology, and attended St. Cloud State for a one year Masters program in psychology and anthropology.

I subsequently left for Europe where, at the University of Geneva I obtained a certificate in Adolescent and Child Psychology. Jean Piaget was one of my professors.

I obtained a scholarship to the University of the West Indies in Jamaica, where I partied too much and failed my exams (another story that I will relate if or when I write my autobiography), I worked in Nassau and met my beautiful wife to be Pauline. I went to England, retook my exams and passed; got married, had a son, attended the University of Strasbourg – where I switched from medicine to clinical psychology, obtained a Doctorate and returned to the Bahamas to work for the Ministry of Health to develop Psychology and Allied Health Professions.

It was at the Sandiland Rehabilitation Center, almost 35 years ago, where I met Mike Neville and formed a professional and friendship partnership.

Chapter 3

PARTNERSHIPS

May your hands be always clasped in friendship.

Opposites can attract...

Racist!

I was shocked when Tim dumped this on me. In fact, the North of England expression, *Gob-smacked,* seemed more fitting! I could have vigorously defended myself, and I guess I could have kicked him out, though he is kind of big, but instead, I swallowed my emotions and asked, "Why on earth do they feel that way?"

"Well, each morning you walk in past the administrative personnel with your head in the air and do not even say *Good morning.*"

The reality was that this was absolutely true. I (Mike) tend to live in a bit of a dream world and I am capable of walking past close friends in the street and not even notice. In addition, I had just returned from England where, unlike the Bahamas, hardly anyone says *Good morning.*

I tried out the *Good morning* suggestion and found that I really liked the response of my colleagues. If Tim had not been brave, honest and trusting, I would have almost certainly failed in my ability to deliver psychiatric services in the Bahamas.

This exchange turned out to lay the foundation for our work

together, but there was more too. While we did not agree on many things, there was and is an almost uncanny similarity in our thinking and ways of working things out. Often these patterns can be explained by growing up together or going to the same church or school, but we seemed to have very different backgrounds:

- Tim grew up in the peaceful tranquility of the Bahamas; Mike in the inner city of Manchester until being dispatched to a Roman Catholic boarding school at the age of nine.

- Tim went to school in Nassau, close to home. Nassau back then had still to reach national maturity and race, color and family name were the order of the day.

- Tim attended the Brethren Church, loved and played music, participated in basketball, cricket and the high jump, finally leaving to study medicine (according to his father's wishes), but ended up studying psychology.

- Mike was fifteen years younger and grew up in the peace and love of the sixties playing rugby and listening to the Beatles and the Rolling Stones, leaving high school to study medicine.

- Perhaps summer holidays were similar, with Tim often returning to his family roots in the Island of Eleuthera and Mike to County Cork where the life styles were of backwater fishing villages unspoiled by the ravages of the modern world.

These thumbnail sketches of two backgrounds could not be more disparate, so is there any other link?

We think we found it, though maybe a bit far-fetched and spun with Irish magic if we travel back in history. Our ancestors can be traced back to County Cork in Ireland. Tim's great grandfather was from Blarney (circled) and Mike's family was from a farm down the river Lee outside Macroom (circled), a simple crow's fly away. Perhaps genetics creep into all sorts of things. It certainly explains how we both got the gift of the gab and it has led us to a wonderful partnership.

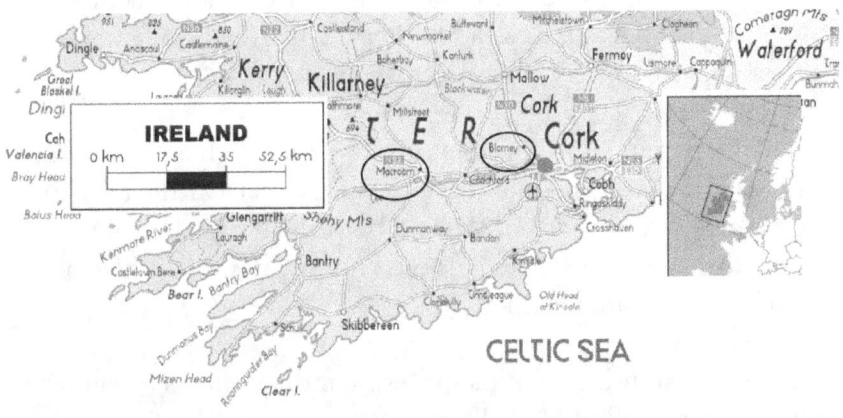

We first worked together in the early eighties when the freebase (crack cocaine) epidemic hit the Bahamas. We joined together to provide educational seminars which provided insights into the societal problems that were both created by and then caused by the effect of the drug abuse epidemic. This work gradually developed into treatment approaches which were based on our concept of the Therapeutic Learning Process (TLP).

A fundamental concept of the Therapeutic Learning Process is the belief in and respect for humanity. Drug programs have frequently borrowed ideas from Alcoholic Anonymous, and perhaps the most abused is that of *tough love*. It is clear that in order to accept that the substance has an immense power over us, we will need a deep sense of humility.

This is often denied and while fellow addicts can challenge denial with some tough or even harsh criticism, TLP is addict to addict. There is no judgment, no condemnation, and it is based on fellowship and encouragement, a far cry from a professional deliberately humiliating a client in the guise of tough love.

It is this respect for each other that should form the cornerstone of all partnerships, whether business or pleasure, along with this regard for oneself, as well as others, which leads to better professionalism and feelings of inner self worth.

Humor also brought us together. It is cruel to laugh at other people, but to laugh about things and even oneself can clear the air and enormously relieve tension. We had both always used laughter in our work and in our lives, so it was no surprise that it began to creep into our work together.

Tim delights in using examples to explain the vagaries of cultural effects on personality. He believes that each nation has its own pet illness. For example, Germans have bad backs, the French complain about their livers, the Bahamians have gas, and of course, the English have hemorrhoids. Tim claims this is why Mike speaks with a posh English accent and sounds as if he is talking with a potato stuck in his mouth!

There was a natural progression from the individual and societal malaise of drug problems to understanding how the business community worked; why some were successful and why most of them failed. People have the same worries and whatever environment we find ourselves, we take ourselves with us. It helps if we know what is happening in the society that we live in so as to get the best out of the workforce.

It seems so obvious that it is hardly worth saying, but we all work harder and better when we are happy and while we would not suggest that it is the employer's sole responsibility to make their workers happy, they do have influence on their employees' lives and it is worth investing in that influence.

We must all take responsibility for our own happiness and decide how hard we are going to work; understanding basic concepts of human behavior helps. I wish we could add hard work to the list of humanity, humility and humor, but that would be less than honest. Ah, there we go, honest, another H which we can add to our partnership.

We have said before that we have never needed a written contract in all our years of partnership and while we cannot recommend this to people in business (in our ever more competitive and perhaps dishonest world), it is worth asking yourself why would you have a partnership with someone that you cannot trust? We do work hard, but it's just not our driving force; nor has the love of money or fame been a prime motivator for us. We place values on other aspects of human life and we are very much on the creative edge, best summed up by a weeklong workshop that we provided for a five star hotel in Ocho Rios, Jamaica.

We were brought in to look at attitudes, negative customer service, and work ethic at all levels of staffing at the resort. It was Mike's first trip to Jamaica and Tim had often enthralled Mike with the descriptions of the vibrant and exciting culture and the beauty of this island. Mike already loved the Caribbean and was a fan of Bob Marley. The downside was that Tim was recovering from an illness and he was under strict doctor's orders to drink no alcohol and avoid all rich food and sauces.

We arrived at the splendid resort and that evening tried out one of the fine restaurants. Mike, sympathizing with Tim, had different wines with each course, asking Tim to smell the bouquets and describing how they combined with the rich creamy and peppery flavors of his gourmet dishes. It was a wonderful night for Mike, but Tim was obviously *suffering*.

The next morning they began with a session for all the front line staff. The room was quiet and the participants were silent, even subdued, and not the vibrant folk that Tim had talked about.

Time for role play. When the lecture format does not work, change! The set up was easy enough; Tim was a porter and Mike a rich, pompous tourist. We said nothing about our respective color that was self-evident by sight and accent.

Mike had mislaid his Rolex and accused Tim of taking it! Tim was meant to diffuse the situation by expressing sorrow that the watch was missing and help the disturbed tourist look for where he may have left it.

No such luck, Tim grabbed Mike by the shirt and shoved him up against the wall in a most undignified manner.

Mike was thinking "Oh dear, I must have pushed the food joke a little bit too far last night," when at that very moment the audience leapt to their feet shouting, "Slap the honkey!" "Hit him!" "Hit the white man, hit him!"

Tim gradually lowered Mike back to a position of frayed dignity and slowly turned to the excited audience and said, "So you guys don't have any racial problems in this hotel?" We all laughed and laughed, and everyone became animated and began to share experiences.

Racial difficulties are still prevalent in our modern multicultural world, but most of us are afraid to discuss differences except within our own closed groupings. This leads to misunderstandings as people have different ways of saying and doing things – ways that can be insulting to others even when no offence is intended. The ability to talk openly can heal so much.

We learned some interesting stuff that week. After that morning session, they insisted that we eat in the staff canteen (local food, not gourmet, but arguably better) to reinforce strategies for change and a chance to *schmooze!*

One of the waiters told us that he discovered he had insulted a number of Japanese guests, completely innocently, when they told him that the way that we beckon guests in this part of the world was the method of communicating to dogs in Japan!

When Tim and I first met and he communicated to me that I was perceived to be a racist, it was a brave man that was able to honestly give me feedback on perceived negative behavior. It started a friendship and a partnership that have lasted a lifetime!

Truth is, we all need relationships as they make up an integral part of our home and work lives. Very few of us are suited for the lonely life of a hermit alone in a cave! We all worry about so many things, but usually it is our relationships that sustain us.

A question that you can all ask yourselves is: "What is causing me most worry?" Make a list, write it down. This list, long or short, often has financial components to it. Even very wealthy people worry about money. Then we ask that you imagine that we have just given you devastating news "You only have three months to live." The question now is, "What do you want to do in those three months?" The answer is invariably about people: who you can see, who you want to spend time with, who you need to talk to. The reality is that no one has figured out how to take their money with them, and so, near the end of life, it is all about relationships. The Pharaohs tried to take their wealth with their gold and fancy pyramids, but that was all scooped up by grave robbers.

A good place to begin your list is with your mother. We are all meant to have one, and sometimes even the most dubious mothers have their honor defended to death. There are obviously things that happen in utero:drugs, infections and smoking to name a few; but we are stuck with that damage when we arrive in the world. We don't remember it, nor can we do much about it.

There is however, a great deal of research into the early mother-child bond and the psychological damage that can occur when babies are deprived of a loving, caring environment. There is now a growing involvement of fathers from very early age which research and good wisdom tells us must be a good thing. These are relationships, however, that we cannot choose. We hold on to them during our lives, often pretending that they were perfect, unable to face the abuse that may have scarred us.

The simplest place to start to resolve the conflict in our relationships is with the reality that none of us are perfect – not us, not our parents. The ability to accept that they were the way they were and it is still okay to love them, even if some of the things they did may have been far from okay, is a major step towards emotional growth.

The difficulty with not accepting this reality is that all other relationships will be compared with an idealistic standard that never existed. A warm, nurturing relationship with our parents makes it much easier to feel love and accept love. Naturally this is a huge advantage as one makes friends and then moves on towards adult family life. It is, sadly, all too frequent that we find adults behaving like small children having a temper tantrum in the middle of a relationship discussion. It is, of course, even more complicated when we add in the rest of the family siblings, uncles, aunts and cousins. Love and hate statements are tossed about: "Who is the favorite?" "Who is loved most?"

We ride around on our imaginary carousel fighting imaginary battles in our heads that are transposed onto fights that range from the trivial to despotic. This ability to carry hurts that end up becoming a part of arguments years and years after the initial hurt, is saddening and scary.

Over the years, we have helped people with all sorts of relationship difficulties from the mundane to the bizarre. The core to so many problems is the ability to listen. It is truly amazing how few people know how to listen to each other. Arguments are built on evidence that is what they think was said or meant and all too often each person has totally different visions of exactly the same event. "I'm right, you are wrong" echoes around the house.

It would save so much emotional energy if we could just listen, not deny the accusation and really try to understand what the other person is trying to communicate. The accusations, which may or may not be true, are often not the real communication that needs to be understood.

Chapter 4

USING YOUR OWN TOOLS

It is a long road that has no turning.

Think outside the box...

Very early in my practice in the Bahamas, I (Tim) realized (as indicated to in other parts of this book) that my professional training for using psychoanalytic techniques was not working. Not only was I becoming very frustrated, but an incident with a patient was so traumatic for me, that I was considering abandoning psychology and perhaps trying to become a musician? a pharmacist? a businessman? a cook?

The lady was 38 years old, just promoted as an assistant manager at an international bank, married with three children, with a husband who was a taxi driver. She was referred to me by my cousin, a family physician, who gave me some background information and thought that she was not adequately coping with her problems. He also believed that she had some 'hidden' difficulties.

"Good," I thought. "With her education and willingness to see me, she may be an excellent candidate for psychoanalysis."

The lady entered my office, very upbeat, neatly dressed, attractive, good eye contact and evidently comfortable as she sat in my *comfortable* chair.

I proceeded with the usual background information which she spontaneously and articulately supplied. Great!! I thought. We then talked about her present difficulties which I asked her to specify and clarify. When the hour was up, I gave her some homework. I asked her to keep an "emotional diary" for me, so that at our next session, I would be able to understand her life and emotional state much better.

Two days after our initial meeting, I got a telephone call from her stating that she was feeling very depressed and needed to see me. We discussed her anxieties. I helped to calm her down and assured her that we would discuss everything more fully when we met for our next session.

The next day, I got another call from her stating that she was feeling much better and looked forward to our next session.

The day before our session, I got a call from her again and this time, she sounded agitated, almost insisting that I see her immediately! She didn't know whether she would live to see me the next day! I succeeded in calming her down and told her that I could see her earlier than our predetermined session since I had a cancellation.

The next day, she came almost an hour earlier than her time and my assistant indicated that she was restless, mumbling to herself and wondering whether I was ready to see her.

What a difference a week makes! When she entered my office, she was agitated, wondered why I didn't see her immediately, whether I cared for her feelings and said that she was feeling miserable. She was standing and, even though I asked her to sit, she remained standing as I sat behind my desk.

"I know that you are feeling frustrated, but here is what we are going to do. I am going to ask you to lie down on the couch over there. I will teach you how to relax and then I want you to just verbalize your thoughts – that is, whatever you are thinking I want you to just talk! Whatever you have on you mind, just say it! This will allow me to better understand your thinking processes and we may be able, after a few sessions, to help you feel better."

"OK, Doctor. I need to relax anyhow." The lady got comfortable on the couch and followed my directions for deep breathing exercises.

Then I asked her to verbalize her thoughts. The session went better than I expected and she even told me of a dream that she had.

Two other sessions went without incident. The next time she came to see me, she was dressed in a very loosely fitting dress. She relaxed on the couch, slightly opened her legs (I guess to expose them seductively to me) and started to talk.

Then she abruptly stopped, tears welled up in her eyes, and she said, "I've decided to leave my husband. I never really loved him I know that you are married, but I know that you want me because you listen to me and seem to be a gentle person. I'm ashamed to tell you this; I'm really confused."

She then pulled her dress down, crossed her legs and turned her head from my gaze. I was not surprised by this *transference* experience. When I met with her and her husband prior to deciding that I would see her for psychotherapy, I explained some of the potential reactions of the psychoanalytic doctor-client relationship. I told her that I understood her feelings and reminded her that we had already discussed the potential of this happening.

She then began to cry loudly and exclaimed "I know what we discussed, but this is for real! I've never loved my husband and I know that this is the first time that I know what love is!"

I explained that these feelings would abate as she began to understand what was really happening to her, that this was a brief reaction and we would try to place this love on to herself and her children and husband.

She then went through a strange transformation. She rose up off the couch looked at me angrily and exclaimed, "Are you stupid? You know how many men want this *pu_ _ y*? I got promoted through this *pu _ _ y* and you are rejecting me?"

She then really lost it. She became very agitated and threatened to *fu_k* me up if I didn't *grind* her.

I had to switch my mode of relating, approached her, and told her that she was desirable, but it would severely affect her getting better if we had an intimate relationship. "I would not be able to help you," I said, "and you would continue to be depressed. Could you just relax, take a few deep breaths, listen carefully to what I have to say and follow my directions?"

At that moment, I really wasn't sure what was going to work, nor did I have any miracle strategy to use. I did, however, remember a technique that I learned from Dr. Maxie Maultsby, the originator of the *Rational Behavior Therapy* methodology. Even though this lady was agitated, I thought I would engage her in some simple exercises.

"Please, just relax. Take deep breaths. Close your eyes and think of a wonderful event in your life. Don't tell me what it is, but I want you to describe the feelings that you experienced at that time."

She slowly calmed down, followed my directions, was quiet for a while and then described her feelings of accomplishments, happiness and joy.

I asked whether she felt the same way while she was explaining her feelings to me.

"Yes, Doctor. I feel calmer now and, the more I think of it, the better I feel."

"Good. Would you like to try something else?"

"Yes, I'll do anything!"

I then asked her to think of a horrible experience in her life. "Don't tell me what it was, but again, explain your feelings."

She sat back for a while. Then I saw her body become rigid, tears filled her eyes and, with a 'sad' look on her face, she replied, "Betrayed, rejected, confused, and angry."

"How do you feel now as you think about this incident?" I asked.

"Angry!" she answered.

I then indicated to her, that, in less than ten minutes, I helped her to manipulate her emotional feelings from feeling *good* to feeling *bad*!

I then said, "Before I do anything else, get back to thinking of another pleasant experience and then we will continue."

Shortly afterwards she said "Wow!! I don't feel as angry as I did. How did you do that?"

"You did it," I said. "I only suggested what you should think about. Listen carefully to what I have to say. We now know that (write this down):
    1. Thoughts always come before feelings.
    2. You control your THOUGHTS.
    3. Therefore you have control of your FEELINGS."

I continued: "Nobody makes you happy or sad unless you CHOOSE to do so. Our emotional feelings are triggered by how we are THINKING or PERCEIVING or ANALYZING events or happenings in our lives. No one makes you feel anything unless you want to."

I then explained to her:
a. The ABCs of emotions,
b. How we function as human beings, and
c. What determines our personality or what make us who and what we are.

I realized that I had changed during that session from a non-involved, somewhat detached psychoanalyst, to a teaching-learning mode. I was showing her, by examples, asking her to participate with understanding, allowing her to be more directive. Because she verbalized fairly well, I used a non-directive approach in collecting information from her.

This worked so well that my patient was feeling better and was prepared to participate fully in her OWN healing. She couldn't wait to experience another session like we had (and she also forgot the *love* talk). I resolved after she had left to begin developing a simple methodology with Mike that we could use, not only for our patients, but also clients in organizations and in our seminar/workshops.

Through research, trial and error, and the results of our approach, we developed a structure – the Therapeutic Learning Process© – but were not locked into it. There were always situations that arose where any structure would not work. The sensitivity of the professional, understanding the culture that has programmed the patient/client, and gaining the attention and willingness to assume control and responsibility for one's own behavior, are goals to be achieved if healing is to take place.

Individuals can usually tell whether their therapist, teacher, or boss is sincere and honest with them. As a professor for many years, students often relate to me their impressions of their other professors. Most of the time, from my personal knowledge of the person they are talking about, their impressions are correct! Professionals, however, should be neutral in discussing other professionals with patients, clients, students or employees.

Chapter 5

THE THERAPEUTIC LEARNING PROCESS©

May the road rise up to meet you.
May the wind be always at your back.

Learning to become your own therapist...

We have previously indicated that our experiences in the practice of psychiatry and psychology in the Bahamas was fraught with referrals that were mostly atypical to our exposure in universities and professional internships.

The manifestation of psycho-psychiatric problems had similarities, but the many cultural factors and the misunderstanding of the population of our professional expertise made it difficult to provide effective, sustainable therapeutic healing.

Mike is brilliant! He has an incisive mind, with an extensive knowledge of medicine, psychiatry and law. His professional interests are in forensic psychiatry, but he is sufficiently visionary to understand trends and circumstances as oftimes shared in his speeches and scientific presentations. These place him light years ahead of his peers, often creating controversies, but also causing people to think. He has an incredible sense of humor and the gift of the gab! He is a person of the highest integrity with a wonderful balance with family, work and play.

Tim has built a reputation of being an effective speaker, professor and an easy-going *gentle giant*, as his family and friends describe

him. He is an accomplished and creative psychologist. He has
the ability to read body language and evaluate situations with a
predictability that his speeches, books, articles and many interviews
with the media seem to have an aura of his being clairvoyant.

—————

We mention this vignette to indicate that we were prepared to think
out of the box and not be afraid to experiment with spontaneous
approaches based on an evaluation of the situation and realistic,
simplistic, caring respect for our patients. Our prescriptions for
change were believable by our organizational clients because of
our proven reputation of honesty and integrity.

Our consultations with organizations, both nationally and
internationally, were remarkable in that there were no highly
structured, textbook approaches. Our knowledge of human
behavior, our ability to quickly adapt to change and our study
of the culture in which we were operating allowed us to provide
reasonable and quick prescriptions that organizations realized
made sense, and which after implementing our suggestions,
worked!

We were sufficiently flexible enough to use traditional
methodologies when there was a need. For example, we used
a psychoanalytic approach with a lawyer from New York who
understood the method versus shifting to a direction-oriented,
charismatic, authoritative therapy for those who were used to
being told what to do, needed high structure and were comfortable
with it. Thus, we began to clarify in a more concrete way what
we needed to do to be more effective and began to develop a
methodology that progressed into the Therapeutic Learning
Process©.

We began looking at research and methodologies that sometimes
developed into theories, philosophies (even theologies) and fads.
We accepted aspects from them that appeared to be sound, useful

and useable. We read many journal articles, attended seminars and workshops, met with many of the innovators of ideas that were written in best-selling books, and provided, through the Bahamas Family Institute, alternative types of healing – acupuncture, hypnosis, transcendental meditation, rational behavior therapy, etc., that had viable elements which could be successfully used. From all of this, we began to see more clearly a structure that provided systematic guidelines for specific problems and a unique way to address them.

Through teaching, providing examples, trial and error attempts, creating an atmosphere of caring and compassion, we found what was effective for developing personal insight and the ability of reinforcing the adage of "client – heal thyself!"

We explored six contemporary approaches that gave us the structure and flexibility to provide simple practical guidance to our clients. What it essentially implies is you learn how to become your own therapist. The professional role can become whatever is required, based on the specific NEEDS and CIRCUMSTANCES of the client. It is not an electic and/or bulls-eye process which usually does not know what the positive outcomes would be. We examine situations and discuss outcomes and alternatives. We realize that there are situations beyond our control, but by and large, we have control of our destiny based on God-given free will and learning from the consequences of our choices and behavior.

This is not a ground-breaking new theory. No doubt many more cerebral professionals and even clients would not feel comfortable because it is too simplistic or too pragmatic.

For all of our seminars/workshops and our psychiatric – psychological practice, we may use the professional "largo" based on intelligence and/or sophistication, but these endowed attributes cause as much anxiety, depression and frustration as do the average, non-sophisticated persons. Also, the only advantage that a wealthy person may have is the ability to change his or her environment at any time. When you are middle-class or poor, with complications of many bills to pay, children to feed and educate, and a relationship that needs to be changed (based on the involvement of lifestyle, pre-nups, community status, etc.), decisions become more difficult.

We based our basic structure on the following theories, methodologies and approaches:

RELIGIOUS-CULTIC-FOLKLORIC-SUPERSTITIOUS

Everyone has some belief system that they value the highest and which motivates them into behaviors to satisfy their needs.

These belief systems are usually part of early programming of psycho-socio-cultural import that provides a value system and the ritual of engaging in behaviors that either conform or do not conform to their beliefs. The impact of Judeo-Christian/Euro-Western beliefs and culture were fundamentally imposed upon those countries that were colonized by European powers like the British, French, Spanish, Portuguese and Dutch. The Americas, (USA, Caribbean, Central, South America and Canada) the vast continent of Africa, Scandinavia, Eastern Europe, and India were all exposed to this belief system that proselytized indigenous (native) people.

The result of the Middle-East, Orient-Asian belief systems, via immigration with Euro-Western ideas, challenged native Muslim, Buddhist, Voodoo, Santeria and the mixture of religions that clashed with the religious belief system of the Mayans, Aztecs, Sioux, Cheyenne and other tribes worldwide.

The folklore/superstitions methodologies of *obeah*, white and black magic and witch craft, have had significant impact on peoples worldwide. The idea of beliefs, values, and practices had to be UNDERSTOOD. How do you treat someone who has become highly neurotic or psychotic, who believes that they have been hexed or fixed, or committed an unpardonable sin, or who feels guilty and depressed because they have broken some cultural codes, or adopted a different religious lifestyle under pressure of being in love or marrying someone of a different faith?

Being unequally yoked was a big problem, especially when more homogeneous societies became heterogeneous and when even laws for whom you could marry were broken. There have been many incidents where a father has killed a daughter who broke an ethic and/or religious code.

Added to all of this, the liberalization of society in re-defining relationships, marriage, adoption; along with the increase in non-religious worship and the pursuit of the "world, flesh and the devil;" were immediate imperatives in motivating us to understand, explore and facilitate all of these complex problems. Our rapidly changing world and especially modern technology have become major stressors with the incidents of distress being very high.

PSYCHO-ANALYTICAL AND NEO-ANALYTICAL THEORIES

The *Collected Papers of Sigmund Freud*, the Austrian psychiatrist, edited by E. Jones in 1950, indicated controversial theories of understanding the human psyche. Freud's development of the id, ego and super-ego; his understanding of human functioning at the conscious, pre-conscious and unconscious levels; and his definitions of "ego defense mechanisms" started the basic structure for what emerged as psychoanalysis and the variations of themes developed by some of his former students and colleagues using neo-analytical approaches.

The theories/methodologies of Alfred Adler, Carl Jung, Henry Stack Sullivan and others, have provided the stimuli for research and more effective therapeutic modalities. The Therapeutic Learning Process© relied heavily on some of Freud's theories which throughout our experiences have been useful in teaching, learning and better understanding human behavior.

HUMANISTIC/EXISTENTIAL APPROACHES

There were many medical and behavioral scientists who thought that the overwhelming, dominating, psychoanalytic approach was too deterministic, inflexible and speculative in interpreting the specific causes and/or approaches in therapeutic methodologies and healing. The writings of Carl Rogers, Jean Paul Sartre, Rollo May, Søren Kierkegaard, Abraham Maslow, Dr. Benjamin Spock, Timothy Leary and many others started a frenzy of postmodern, existentialist, twentieth century philosophies. The exploration of motivation theories, the impact of psychedelic drugs, new musical explorations, forays into Eastern theologies and philosophies, minority discrimination and deprivation – all caused disruptions in societies worldwide.

The protests against the Vietnam War, riots at Kent State University, the Democratic Convention in the 60s, the *make-love-not-war* writings of Camus, François Sagan, the *avant-garde* movies coming out of Europe, Woodstock, and the flower children brought about very exciting times.

Methodologies included non-directive theories, Primal Scream, various sexual theories, alternative medical healings. The advent of more accepted non-legal drugs – LSD, marijuana, and cocaine – was cause for both elation and confusion! It was a giddy, experiential period that was totally opposite to psychoanalytical theory and impacted the enhancement of situational ethics.

NEURO-PHYSIO-BIO-CHEMICAL EXPLORATIONS

Scientists have always been interested in the mind/body connection and in general, realize that our moods or thought processes which originate in our brain are still far from being fully understood. Mapping the brain has brought many advances. We see the practical effects of the psycho-somatic and somato-psychic continuum.

The more recent discipline of neuroscience has been fundamental in understanding the transduction of thoughts into actual physiological responses that can be measured. The understanding of stress, in particular, has been benefitted by becoming more stress – management specific. Also, the ideas of wellness, preventive medicine, nutrition, and lifestyle have been strongly impacted by the findings of neuroscience research.

BEHAVIORAL APPROACHES

Russian physiologist Ivan Pavlov's experiment with having dogs salivate to a conditioned response of ringing a bell at their feeding time, was thought to be a panacea for behavioral scientists who needed a more specific assurance that individuals could be re-programmed to avoid inappropriate behavior and replace it, over a period of time, with appropriate behavior.

The idea of conditioning allowed researchers like Skinner, Wolpe, Bandura, Ellis, Maultsby, et al, to develop methodologies and to try quantifying personality traits that had a more reliable predictability.

Hans Eysenck with the *E.P.Q. Test* of introversion-extroversion, Raymond Cattels (1946) with the *16 Personality Factors*, the University of Minnesota with the *Minnesota Multiphasic Inventory*, Binet's (France) Intelligence tests with a definable I.Q., instruments that could explore the brain (EKG) and the body (sonograms) were useful additions to providing more accurate diagnoses and that took psychology to another level.

The major four behavioral approaches are:
  a. Classical Conditioning
  b. Operant Conditioning
  c. Observational Learning
  d. Cognitive-Affective Learning

We also examined some of the earlier innovative research of the following experts.

1. Walter B. Cannon (1932), *Fight or Flight Syndrome*
2. Desmond O'Neil (1960), *Psycho-somatic Medicine*
3. Hans Seyle (1974), *Eustress-Distress and the General Adaption Syndrome*
4. Friedman and Rosenman (1974), *Diagnostic questionnaire to determine one's susceptibility to coronary illness*
5. Kasanatsu and Herai (1966), *Meditation and brain-wave changes during the meditative state*
6. Adler, Oinestein and Sobel (1987), *The chemical basis of communication between the mind and body; healing effects the mind can have on the body*
7. B.F. Skinner (1948), *Operant Conditioning*
8. Albert Bandura (1963), *Social Learning and Personality Development*
9. Maxie Maulsby (1984), *Rational Behavior Therapy*
10. Albert Ellis (1974), *Rational Emotional Therapy*

LEADERSHIP THEORIES / METHODOLOGIES

Leadership is "an attempt to influence" (Hersey) and a basic component of the human condition since all of us, one way or another, try to get people to do things for us. Leadership of followers, groups, organizations and countries was recognized as critically important and the need for understanding the concept, its development, the skills and styles, initiated a frenzy of research, starting in the late 1940s and continuing to the present.

Trait, Humanistic and Personal-Behavior Theories (especially the Ohio State and Michigan Experiments) essentially indicated that there were two basic styles of leadership - TASK ORIENTED or RELATIONSHIP ORIENTED.

The study of these variables by Blake and Mouton, examined variations of these two dimensions. They developed a

MANAGERIAL GRID, and their workshops would train individuals to develop into *9.9 persons*, i.e. high on-task and high on-relationship skills.

Subsequently, more researchers found that there were many other variables that were significant in the manner by which leaders led!

Situational Leadership Theories were postulated using descriptions such as *authoritative, democratic, laisse-fire, charismatic,* and *transformational,* to name a few.

Situational methodologies and approaches appear to obtain their basic premises from *Fiedler's Contingency Model, House's Path-Goal Theory; Reddin's 3-D Model,* and the Hersey-Blanchard *Situational Leadership Model* and *Leader Member Exchange.*

From these pioneer researchers have come many tests to determine the traits of leadership, structured pathways to effective leadership, and definitive methodologies of highly structured rules and regulations for effectiveness.

The authors have carefully examined the majority of these methodologies and conclude (with biases), that Hersey's *Situational Leadership* has had the longest sustaining power of successful training. worldwide with more than ten million people have been trained in *Situational Leadership.* The Center for Leadership Studies is continually developing modalities to conform to technology and forays, not only into organizations, but utilizing their methodology for parents, teachers and others in positions of authority.

The readiness of employees, children, spouses, and followers, determines the appropriate style of the leader, facilitator, parent, and school teacher.

In addition to extracting methodologies that worked and were non-culturally biased from the previous six approaches, we examined two more areas to complete Therapeutic Learning Process©:

A. ***The Environments in Which We Function***
B. ***Understanding Basic Concepts of Human Behavior***

Let us examine these factors:

A. The Environments in Which We Function

Essentially there are three environments in which human beings function:
1. Intimate
2. Workplace
3. Leisure
   a. Renewal
   b. Sharing

We understand that most individuals have difficulty in maintaining a balance with these environments. A lot depends on their stage of development, career issues, socio-economic levels, belief systems and the ability to ADAPT to situations beyond their control.

We also know that there are CONSTANT displacements from one environment to another, whether consciously or unconsciously.

A person's values has a major effect as to how one *manages* these environments. The three most important skills to deal with these environments are: effective communication skills, conflict management skills and realistic problem-solving and decision-making skills.

The understanding of ego-defense mechanisms and the levels of maturity achieved by a person, provides the tool to find an effective balance in these environments and the ability to adapt to change.

1. Intimate Environment

This environment appears to be the one that holds the highest value for individuals. It includes parents, siblings, family and close friends. This environment is supposed to be one's comfort zone where, after a hard day's work, one can relax in a secure place, be oneself – wear whatever clothes you want to wear, eat whatever food you have, and just chill in your favorite place of comfort.

This environment is important for roots, affinity, status, security and intimacy.

2. Workplace Environment

An individual's educational attainment and job experiences actualize one's career development. This is usually the major income-producing environment which requires people skills, adaptation to the workplace, managing stress, conflict, and being able to increase one's learning and career development.

The age of technology has placed a different spin on how business is done. Information technology and computer viability are essential in modern day organizations. For younger people, this provides a competitive edge over older ones. Yet, experience, vision and structured decision making processes provide a sense of security for older people.

The stressors of poor interpersonal relationships, favoritism, overload, underload, lack of managerial and supervisory training, layoffs, recessions, competition, government rules, and regulations, and the economy are all significant. These factors can also be displaced onto intimate and/or leisure environments. Unfortunately for work-a-holics and others who believe being good to oneself is a waste of time and money, they often find themselves in a state of distress or serious burnout.

3. Leisure Environment

This environment is not only the glue that holds the person's balance in the other environments, but recognizes two basic sub-components:

a. Leisure – Renewal

All human beings need the time to feel good about themselves and engage in activities that provide comfort, strength, motivation and good quality of life. Hobbies, sports, indoor and/or outdoor activities, socializing with friends and family, exercises, diet and nutrition are all valuable in providing the mind/body experience to fuel-up.

The Therapeutic Learning Process© emphasizes leisure-renewal. The lack of renewal can trigger an imbalance that may be a major cause for the inability to function adequately in the other two environments.

b. Leisure – Sharing

"No man is an island." We live in societies where the sharing of one's time, talent or wealth is good not only for the community, but are essential aspects of society that bring people together whether to worship, as in church, synagogue, mosque or any religious/spiritual gathering.

Service clubs like Rotary, Lions, political affiliations, interest and friendship clubs, or being involved in community crime watches, condominium boards for example, are important for sharing and well-being. This is a non-profit sharing of self in helping to support and stabilize the community in which we live.

The Therapeutic Learning Process© examines these three major environments to help the individual find BALANCE in them, so fewer negative displacements can occur.

We know from our patients' and clients' experiences over the years, that constant reality testing and upgrading of knowledge (because of constant change) bodes well for good physical and mental health, and a better quality of life.

B. Understanding Basic Concepts of Human Behavior

All living entities engage in behavior. Over the years countless approaches to understanding human behavior have been developed in schools of philosophy, theology and psychology/anthropology to clarify what makes people tick!!

Most textbooks on organizational behavior supply a simple formula that emerged from the research of Kurt Lewin in the early 1930s: Behavior is a function of an individual interacting in an environment. This became more interesting when the behavioral school developed operant conditioning with which one could almost predict and/or change behavior by manipulating the environment. If we were to expand this formula we can assume that organizational behavior is the function of individuals and groups interacting in an organizational environment (or culture or climate).

Examining approaches, theories and methodologies that we have previously postulated, the authors needed to SIMPLIFY this collective knowledge by teaching and discussing these three basic concepts:

A. *Determinants of Personality*
  what makes us who and what we are
B. *Human Functioning*
  what we now understand about human psyche and the approach to healing, modifying and/or changing unacceptable behavior to appropriate behavior
C. *Feelings*
  exploring factors that have the greatest effect on beliefs, values and behaviors

Most textbooks, practitioners and other interested individuals describe two essential factors which determine one's personality: hereditary and environment.

We, the authors, accept these two factors as essentially important, but we believe that, especially as adults, the aspect of CHOICE is another extremely important factor.

Let us examine these factors:

A. Determinants of Personality

  1. Heredity (Genetic Factors)

We live in an exciting age where cloning, mutants and robots are common. But for human beings, we still depend on the ability of sperm and egg to be fertilized into a fetus that grows into a human being. We believe therefore, that we receive traits or pre-dispositions from maternal and paternal genes. Individuals, without any effort on their part, are saddled with a genetic inheritance which gives them familial patterns of

strengths and weaknesses of behavior and outcomes.
It is important for us to understand our roots (or inherited
genes) and to observe behavior that emerges in consistent
fashion from fathers, mothers, uncles, aunts, grand-parents,
etc., on both sides. Research has definitely indicated that
physiological as well emotional factors are inherited.

My (Tim's) interest in and dedication of my life work to
understanding the human psyche and behaviors, was the
result of understanding some of the major negative factors of
depression, alcoholism, diabetes, and also positive factors of
creativity, music, perseverance, ambition, and spirituality in my
family.

2. Environmental Factors

We have all been socialized after being born, and this
programming allows us to react internally and externally,
whether appropriately or inappropriately, to being comfortable
in our preferences. These factors are our CULTURE, which all
living beings have.

Family practices and traditions, weddings, funerals, religious
customs, folklore, superstitions, ethics, values, languages, food
are all part of this socialization process.

It is more important, however, to realize that all human
beings have the same basic needs: physiological, social and
psychological. The only difference is how we satisfy those
needs. For example, we all go through the cycle of sleep. Some
people sleep in beds, some people sleep on the floor, on mats, in
cars, in huts, in mansions, under tents. We all sleep; where and
how we sleep are individual circumstances, but we still must
sleep.

Food is highly cultural, although travels, the availability of
different foods, specialty shops, and exposure to cooking

shows have provided the average person the opportunity to experiment with many varieties of foods that were not in their cultural experience.

The manner by which we eat food is also cultural. The majority of people in the world eat with their hands, but chop-sticks are used by millions of people. Knives and forks are common to European and the Western world, but there are variations on the themes of knives and forks as well. It again is important to understand these are aspects of culture.

3. Choice

Choices are decisions that we either spontaneously or intentionally make about our lives.

All choices have consequences and it is through these consequences that we learn, change, and/or modify our behaviors.

The process of choice involves learning from experiences, trial and error efforts, problem-solving, and decision-making.

Choices are extremely important because when we examine hereditary and environmental factors, we realize that we do not have to be permanently locked into any of them!

For example, we have the medical, psychological and technological expertise to change and/or modify any number of those factors. If a person does not like their nose, cheeks, color, hair, etc., they can have them fixed. Even our sexuality can be changed over a period of time by medical and psychological interventions.

Our socio-economic levels can be altered by education, hard work, creativity, talent, or luck (winning the lottery).
It is fascinating to read about the many poor immigrants in a

country, not able to speak the language, not a part of cultural programming, often, without a proper place to live, who, over the years, became rich and famous. Poor boys and girls, who through hard work, athletics, music, or beauty, became multi-millionaires, with private planes, huge mansions, and the adulation of people world-wide.

Choices, therefore can override, to a great extent, genetic and environmental factors.

B. Human Functioning

The ideas about levels of human functioning were made prominent by the speeches and writings of Sigmund Freud.

Modern research has explained (or refuted) in more detail Freud's original ideas.

The emergence of neuroscience research has been more precise in helping us understand, especially, the mind/body connection.

We have recognized three levels of human functioning: conscious, pre-conscious, and sub-conscious.

1. Conscious Level:

   a. Immediate awareness of the individual to what is taking place, made possible by the brain and sense organ systems.

   b. The *here and now*; being involved with immediate events.

   c. The integrity of the appropriate function of the brain and sense organ systems essential for our *awareness*.

2. Pre-Conscious Level:

These are remembered or recalled events that continue to affect how we think, feel and act. The *once bitten-twice shy* concept plays an important role as to whether the person has learned from experience. Personality traits play an important role in this learning process because some individuals, although consciously aware that decisions must be made, continually make the same mistakes.

We believe that the next area of functioning, the sub-conscious, may play a significant role.

3. Sub-conscious Level:

   a. The repository where everything that has happened to us since conception has been stored.

   b. We can't remember, but we are still affected in terms of feelings and how we act in certain situations WITHOUT understanding why.

   c. Scientists used to think that to change or modify human behavior, it was necessary to explore the subconscious in order to uncover the trauma that caused the inappropriate behavior.

   d. We now know that the majority of our behaviors are LEARNED and we can at the CONSCIOUS level, modify and/or change our behaviors.

The Human Functioning concept can best be demonstrated by the this diagram of consciousness using the iceberg effect:

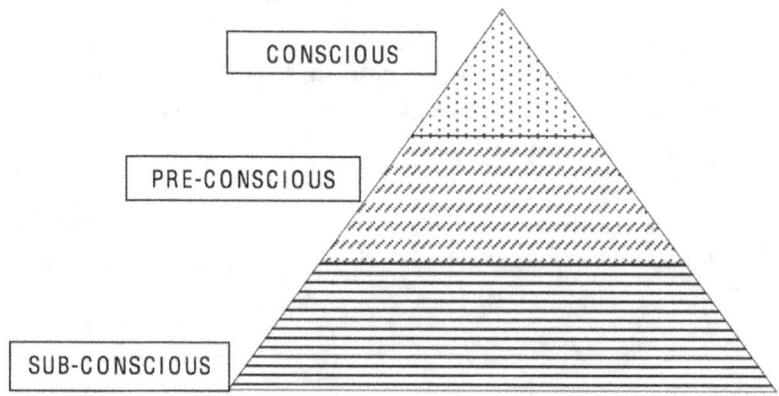

- The *tip* of the iceberg (conscious) is our immediate awareness.

NOTE: Much has been written on the conscious which will not be enlarged in this book, but simplified for better understanding.

- The neck of the iceberg, (pre-conscious) the area straddling the open edges of external and internal depth of water, varies with the level of intelligence, education and insight in reflecting and recalling events.

- The body of the iceberg, (sub-conscious) which is totally submerged and which is not seen, except via sonar instruments, is not only the center of learning but is the repository of everything that has happened to us. As important as it is to explore the sub-conscious, whatever assumptions that a professional makes must still be developed into some process for change. Scientists used to believe that to change or modify behavior, it was necessary to explore the subconscious. Many methods such as free association, dream analysis and hypnosis were used to tapinto the subconscious. This was not only time consuming and expensive, but if assumptions were made as to the cause of behavior, it was still necessary to go through a re-educative process to change or modify those behaviors.

We focus more on understanding conscious and pre-conscious levels to provide more effective, realistic and pragmatic change.

The most important aspect of the Therapeutic Learning Process© is to share what we know about feelings as they are fuel of what initiates our behavior.

C. Feelings

Feelings are part of our human response and they can range from mad and sad, to excited and glad.

There are essentially two types of feelings: physical and emotional.

1. Physical Feelings

    These are stimulus-response reactions made possible by the brain and sense organ systems. In spite of this, through the workings of will power and discipline, we have some measure of control!

    How individuals react to physical stimuli is determined by hereditary, environmental and personal choice factors.

2. Emotional Feelings

    Emotional responses are the result of personal evaluations (analysis, perceptions) of events and happenings in our lives.

For many years, scientists were not able to describe/find the center of people's emotional responses. The evolution of neurology and neuroscience and other/biochemical studies have now been able to pinpoint our emotions that are centered in the Limbic system, where hormonal systems, triggered by the person's evaluation ability (as carried in the neo-cortex system) are transduced into physiological arousal and responses that can be measured.

The manner by which stressors are evaluated, analyzed and perceived gives a person his or her emotional responses.

Individuals are often surprised by the fact that their depression, anger, motivation, frustration, etc. are caused by themselves. While it is true that others may try to influence one's feelings and behavior, persons will feel and react how they have been programmed to react, or, after going through an evaluative or analytical process, make a choice. In considering how this process works, it is important to remember that:

a. Thoughts come before feelings (emotions).

   We can think (fantasize) about anything!

b. We alone control our thoughts.

   When we lose control of our thoughts, we become psychotic and are in need of supervision.

c. Therefore, we alone control our feelings (emotions).

   For further expansion of this important concept, we suggest the writings of Albert Ellis (1979), Biblio (1984), and Maxie Maultsby (1976).

The ABC's of emotions may be demonstrated by:

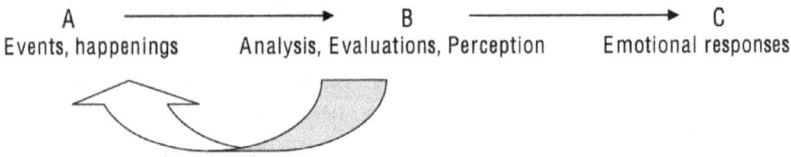

A ⟶ B ⟶ C
Events, happenings   Analysis, Evaluations, Perception   Emotional responses

The manner in which we perceive, analyze or evaluate the events or happenings in our lives triggers our emotional responses. It is never the event of itself that gives us our emotions. It is how we analyze, evaluate or perceive the event.

There is also the concept of cognitive dissonance or mixed feelings. These have been described as *watching your enemy drive over a cliff in your new Mercedes-Benz!* Dissonance is a major cause of distress. Rational thinking, over a period of time, can eliminate dissonance.

In any given situation, one should always remember that **there is never just one way to think, feel or act.** There are always alternatives that the individual can choose.

Overall, it is best to remember that:

1. We can, through choices, modify and/or change factors that determine our personality.

2. We acknowledge the importance of the sub-conscious, but we can adequately modify and/or change behaviors at the conscious (awareness) level of human functioning. Hard working professionals have neither time nor inclination to probe beneath the surface. They want quick, reliable alternatives, and there are processes to achieve these and to maintain balance.

3. We have some measure of control over our physical feelings and almost total control of our emotional responses.

4. By rationally examining the three environments in which we function, a person can make rational decision/choices with regard to these environments.

5. Professional behavior, especially in people skills, should be consistently, appropriately, and positively used in ALL of the environments in which one functions.

6. Coping skills at any transitional stage of development, if followed by applying these concepts, can minimize trauma, irrational behavior, and disruption of family and/or work.

7. A vibrant spirituality, respect for human-kind, and positive mental attitudes often eliminate the boredom/humdrum of life.

8. Awareness of the many stages that we go through, understanding these concepts, and applying these skills, can provide the tools to help people actualize their potential, and find an all-encompassing, growth-enriching life.

Chapter 6

INDIVIDUAL CHALLENGES

*May the saddest day of your future be
no worse than the happiest day of your past.*

Understanding frequent problems that can make us ill...

We all face the world, our work and our relationships as best as we can, but sometimes there are problems that occur that are just a too much for us to handle. The primary problem is illness. Our bodies at times are unable to cope with the everyday needs of life.

There can be no doubt that our bodies are incredible. Just living each day is a small miracle: breathing, heartbeats, eating and sleeping. These daily processes are bombarded with potential pitfalls: infections, organ difficulties, reactions to foods and toxins, etc. Our bodies are constantly fending off outside attack, but, at times, it is too much and we fall sick.

Major medical illness is usually greeted with great sympathy. Family, friends and coworkers gather round, flowers are sent, and most people feel they know or understand something about the illness. There is even understanding from the boss while it is figured out how long you will be off work. We do not need to talk further about this because of this general acceptance of such problems.

There is, however, no such acceptance of so-called mental problems. There is still worldwide stigma, prejudice and simple plain ignorance about mental problems that extends right into the health planners and health insurers to prevent acceptance and understanding of these issues!

The obvious fact is that our heads and the brains inside them are a very important part of our bodies. In fact, it is the part that has some degree of control over the rest of our bodies. So, if something is out of balance in our brains, then other parts of our body will go out of balance as well, which can lead to illness.

Eastern medicine suggests that illness comes as a result of energy imbalance, regarding the body as a fully interconnecting system that needs everything else in working order. This is a helpful place to start.

We, of course, already know this. Isn't it amazing that we can go from sweet air conditioning or the friendly warmth of central heating to whatever the weather wants to throw at us with temperature changes of thirty degrees or more, and our bodies remain at exactly the same temperature?

We cannot tolerate our bodies' temperature being out of balance. If our body temperature went up by just five degrees we would lie in bed dreading the arrival of the grim reaper. It is this ability to worry about things that we will talk about first, a problem that causes endless suffering and countless hours of lost productivity. Like so many other mental health illnesses, it has a name that, while somewhat descriptive, also has everyday meanings that are not quite the same.

Anxiety Disorders

Most of us have some anxiety, but that is not the same as the crippling illnesses that affect about one in six of the world's population – a huge number of people. These disorders seem to stem from a maladaptive stress response.

If you took any high school biology, you may remember something called the fight or flight response. This is the body's mechanism preparing it for stress. Basically, there first must be a thought, an awareness, of some threat or stress. The brain then sends a message to the adrenal glands, which sit on top of the kidneys. These then secrete two hormones, adrenalin and cortisol.

Adrenalin increases the blood pressure, increases the heart rate, takes blood from the gut and the capillaries and concentrates it in the brain and muscles. It also dilates the pupils and increases the breathing rate.

Cortisol also increases the blood pressure and changes stored energy into glucose for immediate use. These changes create those all too familiar feelings of butterflies in the stomach, cold sweaty hands, tightness in the chest and racing heart. This is great if you are about to run the one hundred meter dash, but pretty useless as you stare into a computer screen wondering how your money has vanished.

This of course worked well back in caveman times you went out in the morning with your club looking for lunch. When you saw it you sprang into action, or, if lunch was bigger than you, you ran like the wind, which it is why it is called the fight or flight response.

Sometimes this stress response can get attached to the smallest insignificant things, setting in motion really scary feelings. It is a bit like a short cut on your computer where you click some icon and there you are, not really knowing how you got there. These anxiety disorders do just that, sending us into the oddest predicaments!

Panic disorder sets the stress response into such a reaction that the body feels as if it is having a heart attack – so real that it is off to the emergency room. The overwhelming fear of a heart attack and a barrage of tests are even scarier. Even after the tests show no heart problems, the symptoms are so intense it is not unusual for people to still dread illness.

In the early days of the AIDS epidemic, we both treated numerous clients who were convinced they had contracted the virus from almost laughable sources: scissors at the barbershop, a stolen kiss, sharing a drink and all sorts of panic-stricken ideas.

Social anxiety disorder leaves scores of people paralyzed at the thought of public speaking or even attending a social event. This is common problem for youngsters who use alcohol to give them Dutch courage.

Anxiety also helps create obsessional thoughts. We all get some pretty weird thoughts from time to time, but we can usually dismiss them when we that they make no sense. Imagine if you could not get rid of a thought that you knew to be silly and it just grew and grew in your head until it took over all of your waking moments, leading to what we call Obsessive-Compulsive Disorder (OCD).

Many people feel that there are germs everywhere. This is actually true, but they do not harm us. With OCD it becomes necessary to wash your hands until they are red and raw, and to shower endlessly. It is as if your brain has a little icon like your computer and this shortcut takes you to immediate panic.

To combat anxiety it is essential to regain control of your thoughts, usually with some form of cognitive therapy and relaxation exercises but sometimes with the addition of medication.

Depression

The name depression is really a terrible name for a terrible illness. We all feel fed up or miserable at times, but these feelings usually do not last for long. This leads to the feeling that we can snap out of it or pull ourselves together.

The illness that we call depression is not like that. It can last for weeks, months or years! The feelings are so bad that they interfere with daily living. Efforts to make it go away simply do not work. The illness is very common, with a lifetime incidence of about one in six people worldwide.

Despite this, it is often not recognized or treated properly, leading to work and relationship issues; enormous loss of productivity, and significant loss of life by suicide.

The cause of this illness is like a jigsaw puzzle. There are many pieces that combine to set off a very real biochemical imbalance in the neurochemicals that pass messages around the brain. Serious life events or even serious illness can set it off. It can be triggered by hormonal changes, including low thyroid levels or the female hormone changes at childbirth or menopause. Some of us are more vulnerable than others because of the genes we inherited or because of difficult early life experiences.

There are many symptoms of depression. Some people with the illness get all of them and some only a few. Most will have a number of symptoms from this list:

- Unhappiness

- Inability to experience joy

- Difficulty in making decisions

- Feeling tired, restless or even agitated

- Eating too much or not eating at all

- Sleeping too much, not sleeping at all or getting off to sleep and then waking in the early hours with your mind in overdrive

- Feelings of inadequacy and hopelessness

- Avoiding people

- Loss of confidence

- Anger and irritability, especially with those closest to you

- Thinking of ending it all, life just not worth living

There may also be significant physical symptoms of depression, including headaches and other pains, or a worsening of an illness already present. It is normal to feel depressed after distressing events such as the death of a loved one, divorce, or as is so common today, the loss of a job. Reactions to such events can range from mild to severe unhappiness, or to mind-numbing emptiness and despair. This helps in understanding that the response or treatment must vary to suit the circumstances.

The management of depression can be split into three major areas. Depending on the severity of the illness and the circumstances, it could be one, two or even all three approaches at once.

A. Self Help
B. Talking Therapies
C. Medication

Let us examine these approaches:

A. Self Help

If you get some bad news, talk about it with someone close to you. Get some exercise and keep active. You may not feel like eating but try to eat, but good healthy food on a regular basis. Avoid alcohol and cannabis. They may both help you relax but they do nothing to solve problems and research shows that regular use can make the depression worse.

Write down the problems and try to find ways to face them. Try to get rest, even if sleeping is difficult and disturbed. Vitamins and herbal remedies can be of help in mild to moderate depression. Educate yourself; there are many useful websites that you can access.

B. Talking Therapies

Simply talking about your feelings can be helpful no matter how depressed you are. It can be difficult to talk to friends about certain things, and sometimes friends find it difficult to be objective. This is when a trained counselor can be of enormous help.

There are a number of specific talking therapies such as cognitive behavior therapy. This helps identify any unhelpful or unrealistic patterns of thinking and teaches how to develop new more helpful ways of thinking and behaving. There may also be support groups or therapy groups that can help you talk through problems.

Talking therapy is usually very safe, but it can have unwanted effects. It can stir up old memories and change how one relates to friends and family. This can be upsetting. Always be sure that you can trust your therapist and that they have the necessary training.

C. Medication

The brain is an organ just like the heart and lungs, but it is an incredible organ it contains millions of cells which interconnect with millions of cells around them. The messages are passed by chemical transmitters from cell to cell. These chemical neuro-transmitters are in short supply in this illness we call depression.

This causes a chemical imbalance that is the physiological cause of the illness. If the imbalance is great it becomes more difficult to correct. The research shows that while a mild depression responds to self-help and talking therapies, a severe depression needs more dramatic action usually in the form of antidepressant medication.

There are a wide variety of medications available and it is important to form a partnership with your doctor to choose which medication may help you best. They sometimes have side effects which range from mild annoyances to serious reactions. There is a vast amount of information on the internet and in many books and pamphlets. Read them and use this information as a building block for discussions with your doctor.

It is helpful to see the illness we call depression in the same sort of way we look at diabetes or hypertension. Small imbalances can be managed by self-help and lifestyle changes, but major problems with blood pressure or sugar levels will require medication to prevent serious medical problems.

Let us examine two of the serious mental illnesses:

BIPOLAR DISORDER AND SCHIZOPHRENIA

These are major mental illnesses which affect about one percent of the population worldwide, an immense number of people. Bipolar disorder is an exaggeration of mood swings. Most of us have good days and bad days, which could be viewed as normal mood swings.

In this illness, a person's mood can range from severe incapacitating depression with real risks of suicide to an overactive manic state with grandiose thinking – ideas flying through the brain accompanied by very poor judgment. People with bipolar disorder are often delightful when you are able to agree with them, but fly into paranoid rage in microseconds when you disagree or try to stop their often bizarre plans.

Schizophrenia is another serious brain disease. It remains unclear as to exactly what causes it. The symptoms include disorders of thought such as delusions, which are false, fixed, unshakeable beliefs out of one's cultural context. They can be paranoid, grandiose or totally bizarre. At times the thinking can be so disturbed that it is impossible to even follow a conversation.

Another group of symptoms are described as disorders of perception. These are problems related to our senses where voices (or smells or visions) are clearly heard by the person with the illness but not by anyone else.

The people with these illnesses need professional help. There are no magical cures, but they can be treated. The symptoms are greatly helped by medication and the quality of life of both the family and the person can be greatly improved by working with trained professionals who can help with many aspects of the illness.

Chapter 7

THE McNEV PROCESS™

As you slide down the banisters of life,
may the splinters never point the wrong way.

A simple approach to enhance organizational well-being...

The McNev Process™ is a holistic and eclectic approach to help individual clients. It helps them understand the need to treat everyone in a humanitarian way; to see how their background, childhood and religious experiences have an effect on their present problems; to understand the nature of the problems to be overcome; and to provide insight and discussion into various behavioral and medical methods to address the problems. This desire to help individuals and families was the backdrop to much of our professional lives. Finding ways to use this in a broader societal way was both challenging and fun.

Our first foray out of the medical model came about as a response to the devastating cocaine epidemic that decimated the people of the Bahamas in the eighties. The hospital did not want to look at innovative methodologies and, as much as we tried to share our ideas, there seemed to be more concern over whether the program was a money maker!

We moved up to Saint Augustine's monastery with its beautiful chapel and buildings on a hill near Fox Hill Village. Monastic life

71

has existed almost as long as Christianity itself. It is uncertain who started this tradition, but many believe that Saint Anthony was the first Christian monk. The early monks lived in caves out in the desert, partly as a protest to the opulent view of Christianity offered by the emperors, but also to grapple with the devil. Jesus was tempted by Satan in the wilderness and overcame him through prayer.

The monks sought to emulate Jesus by overcoming their own temptations, which, according to early writings, were remarkable by the lurid and exciting content described. This form of total isolation, as suggested by Saint Anthony, was gradually replaced by a gentler monasticism. The monastic tradition grew with the Irish monks carrying the tradition of rigid discipline south and the Roman monks bringing a more gentle tradition north.

In Nassau, the monastery was founded by Benedictine monks. They came down from Saint John's in Minnesota and followed the teachings of Saint Benedict of Norcia (480-547), who established the rule of Saint Benedict.

The monasteries provided farms, schools, hospitals and places of refuge, and even asylum for those in need. It was that concept of medical care and asylum that seemed to be an ideal match for our clients addicted to cocaine. It proved ideal. We could provide our psychiatric and psychological skills to people living in the monastic community. It enabled us to challenge a common misconception of many drug treatment programs.

The ideas of rock bottom, humility and tough love are a key part of help from fellow addicts, but all too often professionals use humiliation and disdain in the guise of therapy. We were able to follow the rule of Saint Benedict, which closely follows the Gospels of Jesus, and remains as valid today as ever. Monks do not live in the monastery to get away from it all, but rather to make a much needed contribution to life in our times by living a combination of prayer and work.

The monastery accepted our clients as guests. Saint Benedict declared: "Let all guests who arrive be received like Christ, for he is going to say, I came as a guest and you received me." The guests are received as unique individuals. It is perhaps the very humility of the monastic community that enabled the guests suffering from addiction to both regain their feelings of self-worth and the essentials of their own humility by observation and example.

The emphasis on intense individual therapy enabled the guests to make journeys of personal growth during their time in the monastery. We used ear acupuncture to address the physiological/biochemical symptoms of addiction and withdrawal and found this to be highly effective. It also saved us from using medication to treat withdrawal and prevented us from getting into the age-old trap of *my drug is better than yours.*

The whole atmosphere of peace, solitude, prayer and work in surroundings that are set so close to nature provide the time and space for clients to review their lives. The need for work is an essential part of monastic life and it can consist of any work that is of benefit to the community. When we tried out the concept it transpired that we did not have many skills that were of help, so we painted rooms. Tim kept taking breaks to play beautiful melodies on a piano, which helped with the peaceful mood. It clearly does not need to be a Christian monastery, given that monks from differing religions share a need for peace, tranquility, prayer and meditation. With the addition of the professional input, it could be just as successful.

The greatest challenge we faced was in Freeport, Grand Bahama when a schoolchild died *because of the smells.* We had worked with many of the companies helping them develop employee assistance programs as they were being torn apart by the cocaine drug epidemic. In fact, many of their more severely affected employees had been helped to overcome their addiction by stays in our monastic program.

The situation so was dire that Freeport had become the center for industrial development in the Bahamas. This created a circumstance where strong smells could hit areas of the town when the prevailing winds changed and, even worse, if it was raining. Many residents had experienced mild to severe reactions to these smells, but they had always been reassured that there was no danger.

Then one day when the smells were particularly bad, terror struck. A child from a primary school who had often had reactions to the smells, collapsed and died in the ambulance on the way to the Rand hospital. The smells continued and children were collapsing, ambulances were flying in and out. Then a senior executive stated that there was mass hysteria. The anger was exploding and we were called to Freeport to see if we could help the companies in the industrial area deal with a rapidly deteriorating state of affairs.

The most important thing was that a child had died. Compassion, humanity and respect were the first necessities. Then we needed some baseline from which to start. It rapidly became clear that the industrial smells were real and alien to the people of Grand Bahama. People complained about them and were very afraid of them. Having grown up in Manchester, Mike recognized many of the odors. It became clear that the unfortunate child's death was not caused by the fumes. This was of little immediate use, as no one would have believed us anyway.

We put together a proposal to address the problems and presented it to all the industrial movers and shakers. CEOs had flown in from as far afield as California and Ireland. The meeting was held in the top hotel. The waiters were asked to leave so that complete privacy could be observed. We conceptualized the largest group therapy we had ever even dreamt of, with town meetings and achievable, goal-oriented outcomes. After we had finished, there was a hiatus while things were discussed, and Tim was asked about obeah. He told the tale of the *Cat Island Curse*.

A young man was plagued with stomach aches.

The gastroenterologist asked Tim to evaluate and treat him. The young man was 26 years old, very agitated, and kept holding his stomach and saying that a demon was inside him, "eating him up." He said he had been "fixed" (hexed). Tim decided to see how suggestible he was in order to plan a risk-taking strategy to help him.

"Stand-up!" Tim ordered.

"Sit down!" shouted Tim and he obeyed. "Stand up! Sit down!"

"Young man, you have a Cat Island demon in you! This is very serious. Sit down, Stand-up. I am going to hold you and hit you three times – once on both sides and another on the back.

"Three times is the law. I need to hit your back with the *Bible* to drive out the evil.

"Bend over."

BANG, BANG, BANG! A thunderous, prolonged and evil smelling FART blew out of his backside.

"AHHH! he exclaimed. "THE DEMONS ARE COMING OUT!"

"Those Cat Island Demons smell bad," said Tim," as he vividly demonstrated what happened for the meeting.

The audience was in tears, we were given the contract, and the CEO who had flown in from Ireland told us afterwards in the Pub that he would never again be able to fart without laughing!

———

The work was new and exciting. There were fears that we could not have anticipated. Some believed that the smells were causing cancer. Also, as one of the companies made birth control pills, it might stop girls from ever getting pregnant. We held massive town meetings to listen to their concerns. We were honest and forthright. We wanted the truth as much as they did. Our reputation as professionals of integrity helped.

We brought in a forensic toxicologist who was able to answer many of their questions and allay some of their anxieties. The power company agreed to stop burning Bunker C oil to reduce the fumes.

The Catholic school moved, and the companies paid for the high school to set up their own air monitoring station. We knew there would be no trust if the companies posted what was in the air. However people trusted the teachers and students to put up on the notice board what was in the air each day.

This was our first ORGANIZATIONAL DEVELOPMENT consultation and the largest ever. We managed to turn around the entire population of Grand Bahama, which was 26,000 people at that time.

Here is the bullet presentation of our simple methodology. It should be noted that whenever we encountered a problem beyond our expertise, we had a cadre of competent professionals who would assist us (or develop with the organization) to generate the prescription for change.

THE McNEV PROCESS™

A. Thorough Knowledge of Managing Organizational Behavior

1. Individual and Group Behavior

2. Systems Approach

   a. Culture

   b. External Environment

3. Organization Design and Structure

4. Technology

5. Diversity and Globalization

B. Skills

1. Knowledge

    a. Behavior Sciences

    b. Management, etc.

2. Consulting

    a. Proposal Writing

    b. Conflict Resolution

    c. Communicating

3. Conceptual

    a. Systems

    b. Visualization

    c. Design

4. Human

    a. Self-Awareness

    b. Integrity

    c. Stress Management

5. Technological

    a. Computer Literacy, etc.

    b. Access to equipment

C. Start Ups and Contacts

1. Employee of an OD Consulting Firm

2. Advertising

3. Reputation/Word of Mouth Referrals

4. Selling Oneself and Services

5. Resources (professionals with expertise other than yours)

D. Hoping to be Hired

1. Schedule meetings with the CEO or the person who has decision authority in the organization.

2. With them *carefully* evaluate and *specifically* determine their concerns, needs and perception of the organizations' difficulties (situations).

3. How do they perceive *your role* as a consultant and what are their expectations?

4. *Fully* explain Organization Development, (e.g. long range; everyone involved; total organization etc.).

NOTE: Usually at this time, the organization will indicate whether they are interested in the process.

5. Write proposal (general) and, if accepted, ensure the following are clarified:

   a. The preparation of organization and preparations of employees for entry of consultants

   b. Tentative dates (meeting with managers)

   c. Consulting fees and how they are paid

NOTE: Ensure productivity will not be adversely affected.

E. First Contact/Entry into Organization

(1) Examine Totally
the Physical Plant

Space/Offices
Temperature
Color/Paint
Toilet Facilities
Drinking Water/Cafeteria Facilities
Equipment/Technology
Department/Demeanor of Employees

(2) Meeting with
Managers/Supervisors, etc.

Watch Body Language
Consistencies/Inconsistencies
Mood; Attitudes Toward Organization
Information on their IDEAL
Situation/Workplace
How do they see change?
How do they view/evaluate their boss?
How do they view their colleagues/morale
Specify at Least 3-5 problems Areas
Schedule Meetings with Employees
Form Manageable Groups

F. Methodology

1. Ask them if they know/are aware why you (the consultant) are there and the meaning of this exercise.

2. *Explain* your professionalism and try to *minimize* their *defensiveness*.

3. Break them up into small groups and have them *discuss* those areas that are problematic for them or "What are *five things* that prevent you from functioning at your *best* in this organization." Have them list them on a flip chart.

4. Let them choose a leader to report, so as to eliminate the fear of victimization.

5. Have them return and review what their group has listed and discussed.

6. Take smartphone picture of all group lists, have lists transcribed, and provide copies to managers. Study the lists.

G. Analysis and Suggestions for Change

If you have time, you may choose the consistent problems and prioritize them during the group meeting!!

You may also ask them to go back into their groups, choose one of the problems and bring back the solutions.

If they see their concerns are being addressed, change is more likely to take place because, *they* have made the suggestions!!

You must then write a **Proposal for Change**. It should consist of:

1. Introduction - Short description of the organization, what they produce and the *need for change*

2. *Explanation of Problem-areas* and how they will be rectified, (i.e. O.D. Methodology)

3. The logistics of your intervention, e.g.

    a. Seminar/workshop

    b. Group development, team building

    c. Conflict management

    d. Communication for problem solving

    e. Changing structure, process, technology

    f. Suggested *dates/types of groups, etc.*

4. Time needed; follow-up; expectations

5. Cost and how you are to be paid

    a. Immediately afterwards

    b. Long-term contract with global costs and payments at a certain time/currency

    c. Retainer, etc.

6. Agreement of methodology, time, follow-up and payment. Leave room for *negotiations*!!

Chapter 8

SOME SOCIETAL ISSUES

May your troubles be few and
as far apart as your grandmother's teeth.

We do not have to reinvent the wheel...

Two of our friends were trying to get sports scholarships for some promising youngsters and the question was asked, "What can he study?"

"I don't know; maybe philosophy"

"What's that?"

"What's the meaning of life?"

There was a long pause and the final question.

"Alright, I give in. What is it?"

Though not intended, this exchange sums up the difficulties that surround our lives.

When does "life" even begin? Is it at conception as many Christian churches teach, or is it when life can actually be lived independently, as the laws of many countries dictate?

It seems that even discussions around these themes are taboo. Why is it so difficult to discuss and debate these issues with scientists, theologians and people from multiple belief systems? It has always struck us as odd that many who are pro-life and vehemently against abortion are strongly for the death penalty and likewise many who are pro-choice are strongly against the death penalty.

There was a time heralded by the excitement of the sixties when mental health professionals, including the authors, jumped into the myriad of problems facing society. There can now be no doubt that mental health was not a panacea, but a lot of the thinking was valid. Many predictions were made and most ignored. Sadly, many predictions of devastation caused by crime and drugs came to pass.

Fear seems to spark irrational thought. The greater the problems in a country become, the greater number of people will turn to mythology to deal with their anxiety. These sacred stories refer back to bygone days with overvalued ideas that *those* days were much better than now. They often rely on myth and symbolically use sacrificial lambs or scapegoats to attempt to solve modern problems.

It is so easy to blame someone else, be they minorities or foreigners. It is easier to encourage prejudice and horrible treatment as if in some way they can appease the gods. We live our lives based on the culture and religious values taught to us when we were small. All too often we let those around us dictate how we live our lives.

The death penalty typifies many of these values. Throughout the Caribbean and central America, where the murder rate is exploding while most other countries are seeing a relative drop in per capita numbers, there is a groundswell belief that if criminals were hanged, somehow magically, society's problems will vanish. Throw in a bit of flogging and we will be well on our way to the good old days or perhaps back to medieval horror shows.

There seems to be little room for rational debate. There is no evidence-based research quoted, just raw emotion. It is back to the

Old Testament's "an eye for an eye." This, as Mahatma Gandhi said, ends up making the whole world blind.

We accept that society has the right to take revenge, but it is just that it cannot be cloaked in *good*. Retribution should not be sold as a solution to complex problems without the supporting evidence.

In fact, the evidence we *do* have indicates that the benefits are limited. Certainly it has a deterrent effect on the dead miscreant; when dead the chain of revenge has indeed ended.

Of course it would help if there was certainty in the conviction. The advent of death row inmates in the USA being exonerated by the science of DNA is startling.

Also, the case in the UK of the Birmingham pub bombers was very disturbing. They were convicted on the forensic evidence that they had all handled explosives. After many years in jail an investigative reporter met with the real bombers and the case was reopened. It was found that if you purchased a deck of cards at the railway station and played cards on the train, your hands would have tested positive for explosives!

The main myth is that the death penalty is a deterrent to others. There simply is not the evidence to back this up. It seems logical that if we do not want to be put to death, it must work, right? However, over years of talking to people accused and convicted of murder, a very different picture emerges.

In the domestic-type killings, the emotions are so disturbed that there is no thought of the consequences and often little attempt to avoid detection in countries without the death penalty. These unfortunates are at high risk of suicide.

The hardened criminal is likely to kill more people to avoid detection. Many others are fueled by alcohol and drugs, making consequences even more elusive.

One odd case in the Bahamas involved a young man who was addicted to cocaine. He was out in a bar and left with an older man who had *money.*

They drove to an isolated area where the older man wanted sexual services for cash. This totally grossed out the young homophobic cocaine addict, who pulled out a knife and killed him. He found about two thousand dollars in his pocket and went on a massive cocaine binge.

Some days later he went for a walk with his girlfriend whom he loved. He bashed her head in with a rock and was quickly arrested and charged.

When he realized what he had done, he was devastated. He had grown up in a fundamentalist Christian church and developed the belief that he must pay the ultimate penalty in order to be reunited with his lover in heaven.

He did little to help his lawyer in the trial and the automatic appeals process, refusing to even consider a diminished responsibility defense. He seemed the ideal candidate for the death penalty-hungry elements of society.

He was read his death notice, and the lawyers put in an appeal to the Privy Council on the basis that he must be mentally unwell as he actually *wanted* to be hung. He remains in prison and has spent five years there on death row. This is considered to be *cruel and unusual punishment,* so his sentence has been commuted to life imprisonment.

Punishments should also have a rehabilitative component, but this is clearly not the intent of the death penalty.

Crime remains a major problem throughout society. A key goal should be to understand the causes and to see what can be done to address these issues. As said earlier, the Caribbean has a unique problem. Rather than look for a return to the Dark Ages, we should be looking at the economic woes brought to the region by outside decisions.

The Caribbean and Central America have been an ideal conduit for narcotic drugs. This trade has in turn helped the local economies. This has also encouraged the gun trade and drawn the ire of the G20 countries that are trying to prevent money laundering and tax evasion. Add to the mix, the protected trades in bananas, sugar and other commodities have been cut. In addition, the region has suffered a huge economic downfall with an ever-rising birth rate, which is not sustainable by the flagging economies.

There is an urgent need for adequate, well-funded research into these causes, to look at what works and what needs work. There is no need to reinvent the wheel. Many countries are having similar problems. There are pilot projects to see if solutions tried in a city like Glasgow, which had similar kinds of gang problems, could work in parts of the Caribbean.

If drugs are at the core of the problem, it is time to look at properly researched, fresh approaches. For example, in Amsterdam there was decriminalization of cannabis (marijuana), which led to a reduction in school use. Seeing fat, stoned middle-aged tourists was decidedly *not cool*. We are not saying we have all the answers, but that it is time to become less emotional and do proper societal research – first in small projects and then expanding the successful programs.

There have been studies suggesting that exposure to lead is correlated to increases in violent crime. These increases only drop some twenty years *after* the exposure to lead stops. If this is true, how many other toxins can cause this damage to the prefrontal cortex and the anterior cingulate cortex? Could, for example, the exposure to cocaine in the Caribbean and Central America be causing similar pathology to the damage caused by lead?

There is even a theory, known as the *Donohue-Levitt Hypothesis,* that has suggested that there is a correlation between the accessibility of legal abortion and reductions in violent crime. This is more of a sociological concept based on the idea that children who are unwanted and unprepared for are more likely to end up in a life of crime.

The most troublesome aspect of the drug wars and the crime explosion is that it has distracted attention from the great things that were happening in mental health in the past forty years. There has been a reduction in enthusiasm and community-based programs for the mentally challenged. Programs for the elderly are being cut back across the globe. The downturn in the global economy has led to a resurgence of fundamental beliefs and get tough on crime attitudes. At the same time, even the programs that research has shown to be effective are being cut.

Modern life is fraught with pressures and frustrations. One only has to watch the news where there is 24-hour coverage of wars (e.g. Afghanistan and Iraq) terrorist attacks, tsunamis, hurricanes, traffic jams, loss of electric power, downsizing, rising health costs, marital difficulties, drugs, alcohol abuse, bankruptcies, corporation failures and organizational confusion. Add to those factors that not only the mind/body must adapt, but this *wear and tear* of constant stress may eventually result in illness.

This mind/body adaptive mechanism due to change which is a CONSTANT factor has been labeled stress. Our reactions to stress, however, are unique to each individual. Also, good things – promotion on the job, increase in the quality of one's life, challenging work, new love, travel, good food and wine, spiritual peace, positive interpersonal relationships, good friends, etc., – cause adaptative reactions of this mind/body continuum as well.

The remarkable factor is that, whether the change is good or bad, the body reacts the same physiologically. Change, therefore, can bring about an invisible pandemic known as *stress*. Continuous and major change can create a strong culture in which core values are intensely held and shared, and where high levels of continuous mind/body adaptation is the norm.

Today's rate of change has been much greater than the past, yet this is perhaps miniscule compared to the changes for tomorrow. Just look at population growth. For the first time ever in recorded history, world population reached one billion in the 1860s. In the 1930s, the population had doubled to two billion, and then it doubled again in 1975 to four billion people. As of 2013, there are over seven billion individuals on earth. Within a decade it should pass eight billion, despite the fact that many couples in developing nations are having fewer children.

Perhaps the most significant development has been the invention of personal computers. This began in the 1980s and has impacted our lives in such a manner that many professionals cannot effectively do their jobs without a computer and access to email or the internet.

Pritchett and Pound (2005), in their booklet entitled *A Survival Guide to the stress of Organizational Change,* suggest that people should accommodate change, align their behavior with it, and use it to their advantage instead of regarding it as an enemy. Pritchett and Pound also state that with today's rate of change, sometimes one just has to give up or surrender to the change.

Another option would be to simply toughen up by developing higher levels of tolerance for adapting to change. And yet, one has to be practical by not allowing distress to take over one's life.

In order to understand how to manage stress, one has to understand what stress is. We are fortunate that this remarkable plethora of research results have led to the development of theories, concepts and management techniques allowing anyone to not only understand the process, but to be stress management-specific! It is also important to become acquainted with other concepts of human behavior, because, as Hans Seyle stated in 1956, "Life without stress is death." The methodology has to be holistic, with approaches that understand mind/body connections.

The concept of stress has its history in the early experiments and writings of Cannon, Seyle, Friedman and Rosenman, Wolff and Wolff, Benson, Holmes and Rae, Oixfeill, Eysenck and Lazarus, to name a few.

The earliest pioneers, Seyle and Cannon, provided the basic framework for the evolving understanding of the stress response. Later researchers pursued their specialties. Hans Seyle was an endocrinologist who was able to study the body's reaction to various stimuli. Although he experimented with rats in the laboratory, he saw many patients in hospital in which he could not find a specific cause for their illness, (virus, germs, etc.) to determine a diagnosis. He labeled them as suffering from a "syndrome of being sick."

It is alleged that Seyle was having an after dinner drink at home with a friend who was an engineer. His friend was working and calculating the stress and strain of certain metals as important information for the construction of bridges throughout Canada. Seyle likened this to the human body as it responds to the many stresses and strains of their internal and external environments. It is at this time that the term "stress" was used to describe Seyle's idea of the human body as reacting to *stress* in a three phase process. This is called the *General Adaptation Syndrome* (G.A.S.).

Phase I is the ALARM PHASE: The body's first reaction to a stressor. This phase is comparable to Cannon's *fight or flight syndrome*.

Phase II is the REACTION PHASE: When the stressor is continuous, the body reaches a plateau and resistance rises above normal.

Phase III is the EXHAUSTION PHASE: When the stressor persists for a long time and the adaptation energy is exhausted, manifestations of physical and/or emotional illnesses and even death appear.

Seyle (1974) also describes positive, energizing stress, as EUSTRESS and negative non-motivating stress as DISTRESS. The interesting phenomenon is that both are experienced the same physiologically.

The first definitive research on stress was done by Walter B. Cannon, a well-known physiologist from Harvard Medical School. He was the first to describe in detail the body's reaction to stress. Cannon experimented initially with cats and the kinds of manipulations he did to them would be condemned today by the Society for the Prevention of Cruelty to Animals.

Cannon (1932) indicated that a reaction to stress could elicit either a confrontation (attack) on the stressor, running away from it, or being in such a state of shock that one becomes immobilized. He proved that the body prepares itself by attempting to get as much energy as possible to the muscular-skeletal system in order to fight or run away. He called this reaction the *fight or flight syndrome*. The body systems that are associated with strength and energy speed up their activity. Those that are not involved slow down and shut down. There are also "surface reactions" like perspiration, pupillary dilation and piloerection (hair standing on end).

These pioneering researchers paved the way for experiments in the USA, England, Germany, Japan and other parts of the world. Most have focused on other causes and reactions to stress, including stressors, physiological and emotional responses, mind/body connections, and stress and disease. There have been explorations to find effective methods to manage stress and the resurrection of ancient methods of prayer, yoga, meditation and hypnosis.

Some examples of ground-breaking research are:

1. Friedman and Rosenman (1974), who identified the relationship between stress and coronary disease. They developed a diagnostic questionnaire to determine one's susceptibility to coronary illness.

2. Desmond O'Neill (1960), a London psychiatrist wrote one of the first books on psychosomatic medicine.

3. Kasamatsu and Hirai (1966), studied meditation and noted changes in brain waves during the meditative state.

4. Hans Eysenck (1988), from London's Maudsley Clinic, researched a cancer-prone personality and a coronary heart disease-prone personality.

5. Robert Adler of the University of Rochester and Ornestein and Sobel (1987), studied the chemical basis of communication between the mind and the body. They focused upon illness and healing effects the mind can have upon the body.

6. Dr. Candace Pert, a neuroscientist and the former section chief of brain biochemistry at the National Institute of Mental Health, recently investigated chemicals that send messages between cells to various parts of the brain and between the brain and other parts of the body.

Hundreds of these brain message transmitters (called *neuropeptides*) have been found that are produced by the brain itself. Pert believes some of these neuropathies are also produced in small amounts by the macrophages – white blood cells that ingest and destroy bacteria and viruses (Squires 1987).

In addition, "the macrophages are attracted to neuropathies produced by the brains to fight off invasion of bacteria. For instance, macrophages will also travel to help combat the invasion. Since relaxation and some forms of visualization result in the production of neuropathies (for example, beta-endorphins), it may be possible to purposefully cause the brain to produce more of these substances, hereby making the immunological system more effective. The result may be less disease." (Greenberg, 1993)

At present, it appears that stress, in all of its aspects, is widely researched throughout the world. The International Congress on Stress, which had its first congress in 1988, was formed to assemble leading authorities worldwide to present cutting-edge research advances.

At the tenth International Congress on Stress in 2000, some of the presentations included:

1. *Crisis Intervention For the Prevention of Traumatic Stress: A State of the Art Review of Outcome Studies* – George Everly

2. *Reducing the Psychological Consequences of Violence: The Assaulted Staff Action Program* – Raymond P. Flannery

3. *An Overview of Microwave Resonance Therapy: EEG Correlates of Microwave Resonnance Induced Relaxation, editatin, and Altered Consciousness States* – Dejan Rakovic

4. *Biological and Electromagnetic Resonnance: Six Years of Research* – Gabor Lednyiczky

5. *Cranioelectrical Stimulation: An Overview of Its Application For the Treatment of pain, Anxieety, Insomnia, Depression, and Other Stress Related Disorders* – Daniel Kirsch

6. *Magneto Therapy-Metabolic Thermodynamic Treatment of Advanced Metastatic Malignancy and Cardiomyopathy: The Role of ATP* – Demetrio Sodi Pallers.

7. *Evidence for an Electrical Circulatory System and Electrochemical Therapy For Cancer and Biologically Closed Electrical Circuits (BCEC) and Qi* – Bjorn Nordenstrom.

8. *An Implantable Device to Treat Parkinson's Disease By Deep Brain Stimulation* – Bridget Murphy

9. *The Electricity of Touch: The Effect of your Heart's Electromagnetic Field on Others, EEG findings and Implications* and *The Freeze-Framer: A Stress Management Training and Heart Rhythm Feedback System for Increasing Physiological Coherence* – Rollin McCraty.

10. *The Preventative Management of Workplace Violence* – Jonathan and James Campbell Quick

11. *Pulsed Stimulation for the Treatment of Multiple Sclerosis and Migraine* – Martha Lappin

12. *Stress and Violence* – Vittorino Andreoli

13. *Psychosocial and Psychological Factors Involved in the Development of Psychosomatic Diseases* – Tatjana Sivik
http://www.stress.org/cong.htm

STRESS: WHAT IS IT?

Stress has different meanings to different people. Its meaning also depends on which aspect of stress a researcher is focusing. Simply, anything to which the body has to react or adapt to can be termed *stress*. Seyle's description of stress is still valid in that eustress describes the good or positive things that happen. Eustress is motivating and can initiate creativity and positive mental attitudes. Distress describes negative de-motivating stress that can often place an individual in a situation of inactivity or inertia.

There are, inevitably hundreds of definitions that can be found in the literature. The most common may be that stress is defined as a response or as a stimulus. It would appear that the most popularly accepted concept of stress is that that there is a stressor(s) (which can be anything) that triggers off or has a response to (stress) either Eustress or Distress.

Research over the years has established this fact: The body and mind are consistently adjusting to balance and equilibration. *Homeostasis*, the term used for physiological balance, and equilibration, the term used to indicate emotional balance, must be maintained. Any change or threat to equilibrium can be either eustress or distress.

This concept may best be illustrated by the following: (McCartney, 2005)

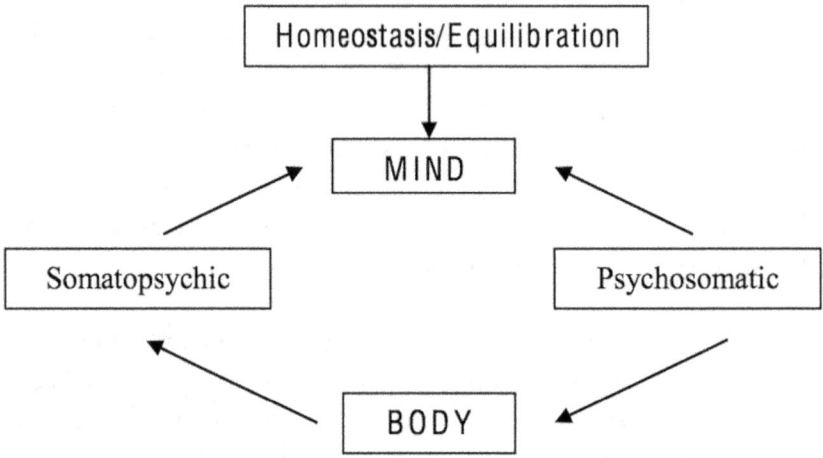

1. The mind/body is in a state of homeostasis and equilibration

2. There is a stressor(s)

3. The evaluative thoughts of the mind cause emotional responses which (emotions) are transduced into actual physiological responses that can be measured.

Here are some psychosomatic response reaction examples-learning of the accidental death of a spouse; being fired from a job; being diagnosed with cancer. The term originates from the Greek words *psyche*, meaning (mind/soul) and *soma* meaning body.

One the other hand:

1. The body/mind are in states of homeostasis and equilibration.

2. There is a stressor(s) trauma to the body which destabilizes mind and body.

3. The effect of the destabilization, if continued, causes mental/emotional states. That is, the body's adaptative processes affect one's mental state.

This is a *somato-psychic* reaction and must be understood in the context that the physiological state of the body triggers, through the evaluative processes of the mind, emotional states that are either eustress or distress. For example, there is an emotional state which results from having a mastectomy for breast cancer. The depression caused by having cancer, the self-esteem issues after a mastectomy, and the constant worry as to whether cancer would come back, can all trigger a distress response.

It should be noted that these are real body/mind states. They are not imaginary or delusional states. When an individual experiences illness for no reason and is constantly imagining a disease, taking lots of medication, and complaining all of the time about their health, this may be described as a *hypochondrical reaction*. The person is usually labeled as a *hypochondriac*.

Stress, therefore, develops when the pressures and demands in one's life exceed one's ability to cope (distress). When the individual is motivated, creative, and able to find balance in the three major environments in which they function, the stress becomes eustress.

Stress has been around from the beginning of life. Even though stressors change with every year and stage of human development, much more is now known about this process. More than 200 million Americans take medication for stress-related illnesses and symptoms. American organizations are losing more than $200 billion each year due to workplace accidents, absenteeism, drug abuse, violence, medical insurance and lost productivity (Edstronm, 1993).

In the United Kingdom, the government sponsored a survey in the spring of 2004 to examine psycho-social working conditions in the British workplace prior to the launch of the Management

Standards for Stress. Areas such as work, alcohol, social risks etc. were studied with recommendations (http://www.hse.gov.ak/stress/research.htm).

The *Neural Immune Program* at the NIH's Maternal Institute of Mental Health (NIMH) has been rediscovering the links between the brain and immune system. "According to Dr. Steinberg, if you're chronically stressed, the part of the brain that controls the stress response is going to be constantly pumping out a lot of stress hormones. The immune cells are being bathed in molecules which are essentially telling them to stop fighting. And so in situations of chronic stress your immune cells are less able to respond to an invader like a bacteria or a virus." (Wein and Harrison 2000).

One should not get the idea that all this is bad because, as previously mentioned, eustress is good for you. Dr. Steinberg further comments (Wein and Harrison, 2000), "The objective should be not to get rid of stress completely, because you cannot get rid of stress. Stress is life, life is stress. Rather you need to be able to use your stress response optimally." (http://www.mih.gov/news/wardonhealth/oct2000storyol.htm)

To summarize what we now know about stress (eustress and distress) the following should be noted:

1. Stress is a neuro-endocrine process that affects the metabolism of the body and has an input on every system of the body including the nervous system, immune system, cardiovascular system, digestive system, the skin and the muscular-skeletal system.

2. A stressor is a stimulus that triggers the fight or flight response. This is comparable to Seyle's Alarm Stage. Stressor and can be physiological, biological, psycho-social, external and/or internal.

3. Psycho-somatic disease is real. It is not just *in the mind* (which is a hypochondrical reaction). It involves the mind *and* the body.

4. Stress-related problems include migraine headaches, backaches, asthma attacks, some cancers, allergies, stroke, coronary heart disease, hypertension, tension headaches, and neck and shoulder pains.

5. Distress, especially chronic distress, tends to make your immune system more susceptible to colds, infections, inflammations, lupus, some cancers and allergic reactions.

6. Stress begins with life situations that become very difficult to understand and which overwhelm individuals in any of the three environments in which humans primarily function (intimate, workplace and leisure).

7. After years of research and the understanding of mind/ body processes, stress management techniques are *management-specific*.

8. Work-related stressors and those internal and external factors that impact employer and employees in organization have been identified. Stress management techniques can restore health and improve productivity.

9. Knowledge, techniques and practice allows for the proper control and well-being of the individual as distress can be transformed into eustress.

SOME PRACTICAL SUGGESTIONS

1. Individuals should try to be consistently positive in all three environments in which they function. A good balance between intimate, workplace and leisure environments causes less negative displacement, consistency and equilibrium.

2. Practice effective interpersonal skills, especially communication and problem-solving.

3. Learn how to set limits to prevent overload. Also learn how to say *No*!

4. Watch your emotional pressure points.

5. Don't waste time feeling guilty about what doesn't get done.

6. Try to enjoy whatever you are doing.

7. Ask yourself if your reaction to situations will help:

    a. Improve productivity

    b. Relationships with others

    c. Is it worth putting pressure on piece of mind and self confidence

    d. Improve overall health

8. Don't sweat the small stuff. Change the way you evaluate situations. Remember it is how we analyze, evaluate or perceive a situation that initiates our emotional responses.

9. Work smarter rather than harder.

10. Don't get involved in routine detail that should be delegated.

11. Attempt to clean up your act. Avoid a general lack of self-discipline, personal disorganization, cluttered environments (desk, rooms, etc.)

12. Practice being an optimist and build on successes.

Research results on stress, psycho-remedial approaches, religious and spiritual cures, and sometimes just reverting to ancient cultural practices have created hundreds of techniques for managing stress. The influxes of Eastern philosophical and religious belief systems have an impact on the Western world and have stimulated other groups to find their cultural healing.

Exploring these methods has given valuable and practical guidelines as to what stress really is. They are more than aiming to hit the bull's eye, but rather to restore the individual to a level of homeostasis and equilibrium in a short time frame.

This approach suggests three basic areas that managers and supervisors can explore in order to understand these processes and to implement a program for effective stress management. The fact is that the stress response (neuro-endocrine) is one of the most damaging and comprehensive physiological reactions that alters the activity of the body's only two regulatory systems. *No organ system can avoid being affected in some way by the experience of stress*. Most of the stress one experiences originates in the mind (psychogenic).

To recap our knowledge of stress psychophysiology there are three linked facets:

1. The functional organization of the human brain.

2. The physiological workings of the mind/body links.

3. The physiological pathways and somatic effects of stress (Greenberg, 1993). The author believes that the better you understand how your body and mind operate, the greater will be your capacity to gain control over your own health.

   To this goal, therefore, three approaches are essential in helping us understand and manage stress. These are:

   a. Analyzing the three environments in which we operate/function (intimate, workplace, leisure).

   b. Understanding basic concepts of human behavior

   c. Exploring the psycho-somatic stress pathway so as to apply a stress-specific management technique.

"The goal is to quantitatively reduce the amount of distress that we experience and to qualitatively change it into Eustress. An optimal amount of stress is healthy and growth promoting. Adaption and stress are essential for life and growth." (Greenberg, 1993)

In order to demonstrate how all-encompassing the stress response is to the physical, cognitive, emotional and behavioral aspects of human behavior, the following table is submitted:

Physical	Cognitive	Emotional	Behavioral
Fatigue	Blaming someone	Anxiety	Changes in activity
Nausea	Confusion	Guilt	Changes in speech patterns
Appetite change	Poor attention span	Denial	Withdrawal
Twitches	Poor decisions	Severe panic (rare)	Emotional outbursts
Insomnia	Heightened or Lowered alertness	Emotional shock	Suspiciousness
Weight change	Poor concentration	Fear	Change in usual communication
Colds	Memory problems	Uncertainty	Loss or increase of appetite
Chest pain or tightness	Forgetfulness	Loss of control	Increased alcohol use, drug and tobacco use
Difficulty breathing	Hyper vigilance	Depression	Inability to rest antisocial acts
Elevated BP	Difficulty identifying familiar object or people	Inappropriate emotional response	Nonspecific bodily complaints
Rapid heart rate	Increased or decreased awareness of surroundings	Apprehension	Hyperactive to environment
Heart palpitation	Distractibility	Feeling overwhelmed	Increased startle reflex
Speech difficulty	Inattention	Intense anger	Pacing
Thirst	Poor problem-solving	Agitation	Erratic movement
Headaches	Poor abstract	Dread	Change in sexual functioning
Visual difficulties	Thinking	Frustration	Low productivity
Vomiting	Loss of time, place or person orientation	The blues	Isolation
Grinding of teeth	Disturbed thinking	Bad temper	Intolerance of others
Feeling of weakness	Nightmares	Nightmares	Lashing out
Dizziness	Intrusive images	Crying spells	Hiding
Shock symptoms	Negative attitude	Irritability	Clamming up
Freezing or "Going Blanket"	Whirling mind	"No one cares"	Lowered sex drive
Fainting	Lethargy	Nervous laugh	Nagging
Sweating	No new ideas	Easily discouraged	Lack of intimacy
Hot or cold sensations	Boredom	Little joy	Using people

Physical	Cognitive	Emotional	Behavioral
Dry mouth	Spacing out	Worrying	
Shallow breathing	Negative self-talk	Resentfulness	
Stomach or intestinal distress	Looking for magic	Loneliness	
Muscle tightness	Loss of direction	Distrust of others	
Muscle aches		Emptiness	
Accident prone		Loss of meaning	
In coordination		Unforgiving	
Foot-tapping		Apathy	
		Cynicism	

Chapter 9

PREDICTIONS

Behold the former things have come to pass and new things
I declare before they spring forth, I will tell you of them.
— Isaiah 42 v. 9

We are all going to die.
That is an easy enough prediction…

Not exactly a delightful thought, but none the less true. We don't usually know the time or the place, but one day the BANSHEE will come wailing. Irish mythology describes the banshee as a female spirit usually seen as an omen of death. It is generally believed that Irish families with the prefix "Mac" in their names will usually hear the wailing of a woman before death arrives. So both of us (Mike's mother was a MacSweeney) may well receive a macabre warning. We are not sure that such a late warning will be of much use, however, as it does not leave much time for preparation.

In an equally gruesome type of warning, a prison officer once told us that the condemned man miserably awaiting his fate, was really very lucky as he did know the time and place that he would die. Therefore he could prepare to meet his God. We really do not think that either of us would want that particular piece of luck, but what can we do?

We can all make choices that can improve our health so that we may live longer. We can choose to improve our lives in so many ways. This will allow us to approach death with less apprehension and hopefully leave a positive energy imprint on planet earth when we depart. Leave we must and leave we will.

It is very important to remember that we cannot take our worldly acquisitions with us. The Pharoahs tried, filling their pyramids with gold. Sadly it was not the gods that were impressed, but the grave robbers who ransacked their tombs years later. Cemeteries do not, as far as we know, accept U-Haul trailers with the coffin. Even if they did, history is replete with stories of even modest graves being robbed.

The most famous case of grave robbing involved men named Burke and Hare, who, realizing the shortage of cadavers in the medical school at Edinburgh University, not only emptied graves but went a step further. They murdered people to supply the needs of those young doctors who required cadavers to dissect to help them learn anatomy. This may sound awful, but it probably led to huge advances in the knowledge of anatomy and greatly improved surgical interventions!

It was not really admired back then as the doctors were thought to be so degenerate that surgeons were banned from using the title DOCTOR and stopped from performing jury duty. In England, surgeons still go by the title Mr. or Ms., but it is now seen as a sign of respect. Most people now believe that doctors are excused jury duty because they are so busy healing the sick.

This must all sound rather morbid, but it is somewhat tongue in cheek and should not to be taken too seriously. There are, however, many mental health predictions that are ignored all over the world. The authors have made more than a few of their own.

Tim started talking about the societal changes that would lead the Bahamas down the path to crime unless the issues were addressed.

He helped establish treatment for alcoholism and worked tirelessly to explain mental problems to the whole Caribbean. He published major books on these issues, most notably *Neurosis in the Sun* and *Ten, Ten the Bible Ten.* He became president of the Caribbean Federation for Mental Health, and was recognized in the Bahamas in numerous ways.

Ball highlight

LADY SASSOON presents Dr. Timothy McCartney with the Golden Heart Award at the Heart Ball on Saturday evening. Dr. McCartney a consulting psychologist at Sandilands Hospital, has helped countless people suffering from alcoholic and mental problems.
PHOTO: Andrew Toogood

Work for alcoholics wins Golden Heart Award

In 1969 he was the recipient of the prestigious "GOLDEN HEART AWARD."

"The Sir Victor Sassoon Heart Foundation instituted this award to be given annually to the person who has given of himself unselfishly to promote human welfare and dignity while making life better for his fellowman. Winner of the 1969 award was Dr. Timothy McCartney, a consulting Psychologist at Sandilands Rehabilitation Center. He has helped countless people with alcohol and mental health problems. Much of his work is done after hours and he gives freely of his time and knowledge in this field."

— Official Program Brochure

———

Tim entered the Bahamian scene in 1967 when he returned to the Bahamas to take up a post for the Ministry of Health to develop the profession of Psychology and Allied Health. He was young and energetic. Even though he had been away from the Bahamas for about 15 years, he often made trips home and was quite *au courant* (current) with the difficulties and also some of the positive changes taking place in his native land.

It is interesting that his first speech was to the Rotary Club of Nassau in 1967. He was asked to describe his profession of Clinical Psychology and some of the problems that he noticed. His speech was only 20 minutes, but during that time, he articulated the urgent problems that he felt needed rational and creative attention.

The questioning session which was supposed to be only 10 minutes, lasted for nearly an hour. When the official meeting time expired, more than 60 percent of the members and guests stayed around to probe this new professional's mind.

After that initial speech, Tim was inundated with telephone calls and requests from civic, religious and political organizations to speak on topics like alcoholism, drug abuse, marriage, depression, sweet-hearting, racial and culture changes, etc. Tim also became a member of the newly formed Bahamas Mental Health Association, and was invited to become a Board Member. He accepted and immediately suggested that the Association needed a Mental Health Week, to not only share the usefulness of such an organization, but also to address the taboos of mental illness and its debilitating superstitions that were a cause of isolation, denial and undue suffering for persons afflicted with the disease. He also wanted to provide a non-biased, rational approach to difficulties facing a new political and socio-economic order.

With Tim's involvement over the years, is just impossible to understand how he found time for his government job, his private consultations, and his involvement with many Associations, his leadership roles, his constant travel, and time for his family. To demonstrate a few of the contributions in his incredible career, cartoons and scripts of some of his speeches will be briefly documented.

There was some controversy with the Bahamas Christian Council when Tim gave a talk on *Religion and Human Sexuality*. The following is the article in the *Nassau Guardian* Newspaper, March 1979 and *Pot Luck* cartoon.

The Tribune, Tuesday, March 6, 1979

Clergy need training in
sex counseling techniques

by Wendy Miller

Members of the clergy need to be trained in counseling techniques in the field of human sexuality and how to deal with people, it was concluded on Wednesday night.

This came at the close of discussions focusing on "Religion and Human Sexuality," held at the Bahamas Baptist Bible Institute, as a part of week-long activities for Mental Health Week.

A short paper was presented by Dr. Timothy McCartney, chief psychologist, Sandilands Rehabilitation Centre.

He stated that the influence of the church is waning, despite the obvious rise in church-goers, membership and the increase in churches being built here today.

"It appears," Dr. McCartney said, "that there is a slow shift in Bahamian attitudes, where mental health professionals, medical doctors and non-religious professionals command more respect and validity than the average religious minister. When there are burning issues in the community, more than likely the politician or non-religious professional will speak out!"

He said it is not known whether this shift in attitude is due to the personal lifestyles of ministers of religion, who have been projecting a hypocritical stance, and are "afraid to stand up and be counted," or because the type of information given by the church is questioned as to its veracity or practicality.

"On the positive side," he said, "and especially with regard to sexual issues and problems associated with sexuality, there are some churches who have spoken out and who are actively engaged in training schemes, counseling services and public information.

"For example, the Roman Catholic Church has, for some time now, conducted pre-marital and marriage courses. It has also held workshops on contraception utilizing the rhythm method and, just recently, the Roman Catholic Bishop wrote a pastoral pamphlet, defining their stand on issues of human sexuality and morality… mainly abortion."

The Methodist Church, he noted, is also dealing with its people, in terms of advice and counseling.

"But the global impact of religious thought, especially on sexual and moral issues and programmes, have not been forthcoming, by and large, from the Church in the Bahamas," Dr. McCartney stressed.

"Surely, the profound changes in sexual attitudes and practices throughout society are raising serious questions about the adequacy of traditional formulation for a responsible sexual life. For example, parents are not always clear on how much their children know or should know about sex. Many parents feel that knowing to much, too early lends to sexual behavior, but most experts have the opposite view.

Children are more likely to have sexual difficulties if they don't know what sex is all about. For the general population of human resource personnel, there is also abundant ignorance, misinformation and an inability for those very professionals to come to grips with their own sexuality."

Wednesday's session was in the form of a workshop, which was designed as an introduction to sensitivity, openness and serious enquiry into aspects of sexual-religious issues that are of prime importance.

"You ministers of religion," Dr. McCartney said, "are the target group of this workshop. We believe that it is vital that you and members of the professions that work with psycho-social and religious problems would find a commonality of purpose and strive for more co-operation with trained mental health professionals.

"There has always been a complexity of Christian thoughts toward sex. The Christian tradition is marked by an historical development extending some 3,000 years. It has been subject to a plurality of religious, cultural and philosophical influences. Although rooted in the Bible, which in itself attests to moral evolution and comprises a variety of theologies, interpretations, which, today, still causes differences of opinion and, of times, confusion.

"This confusion is to be understood in light of understanding the limitations of prescientific knowledge of biology, religious taboos and superstitions, the tradition of subhuman treatment of women and a dualistic philosophy of human nature. Sexuality should not be studied in isolation. Unless it is seen as integrated into the whole of human life with all its relationships, sexuality can too easily degenerate into naïve biology or moralistic inadequacies. Human sexuality has to be approached with the help of the Holy Spirit, which guides and directs us, but also in the context of Christian anthropology, modern research and biblical and classical anthropology."

To recognize God as Creator and Lord is to acknowledge human creatureliness and dependence, he said. The human spirit, while related to the divine, is not identical to it.

"There is no disparagement of the body as if it were evil or inferior. We are living beings that God has created in his own image, with the ability to think and communicate our thoughts. The gift of thought – intelligent thought – makes us higher than sub-human animals. Because of these indisputable facts and the complexities of human programming it would be foolhardy to make simplistic judgments regarding imputability. Serious consideration must be given to various subjective factors that can profoundly interfere with and affect the objective – ideal moral response."

The modern pastor, he said, or theologian, minister, priest, or whatever, must be sufficiently motivated to grow both theologically and scientifically.

"There is no excuse in this present day Bahamas for ignorance," Dr. McCartney said, "or for putting one's head in the sand. Surely, if nonscientific and scripturally misinterpreted advice is given to rational thinking human beings, that pastor or priest not only is doing a disservice, to his parishioner, but also violates the natural and religious laws of God."

Human sexuality, Dr. McCartney said, from a holistic or total approach, must be looked upon in terms of a definite theology, which would explore areas such as the definition of sexuality; the principle of integration for the various purpose of sexuality and the moral evaluation of sexual conduct, in addition to the empirical sciences and human sexuality.

"There has always been a discrepancy between observed religious principles of rules and the actual behavior of its adherents.

"For example, the Christian church only sanctions sexual intercourse within religio-legal marriage. Statistics indicate, however, that the majority of people do not adhere to these rules. You know, as well as I do, that a significant number of brides are pregnant before marriage and you also know how many of your faithful, God-fearing members, engage in sexual intercourse before marriage, as well as while married (that is, committing adultery)."

An approach into the last method would require looking at sexual behavior from all angles, he said, including seeing whether there is a specific behavior universally prohibited by all cultures; the sexual behavior of animals, in contrast to human beings and, he said, there is a need to view issues that still cause confusion, such as masturbation, premarital sex, abortion, the role of love in sex, divorce-remarriage, and sexual practices such as oral-anal sex and flagellation.

Once small groups separated and discussed the topics above, the consensus was mixed.

It was also mixed on what would happen to a young girl, who is a member of a church, very active and gets pregnant.

More speeches of various topics – were made sometimes with *tongue-in-cheek*, although the predictability was not that far-fetched, as was depicted in the next cartoon.

Nassau Guardian, Tuesday, June 15, 1982

Tim also commented on *promiscuity* which got this response.

Nassau Guardian, Friday, May 1, 1981

And again talking about the males' mid-life crises: "There is no fool like and old fool"

Nassau Guardian, **Thursday, June 18, 1981**

Mike came on the scene a bit later and became very concerned by the upsurge in drug abuse in the Bahamas. The seven hundred islands have always provided a refuge for pirates and smugglers, and it provided the ideal geographic conduit for the transport of drugs from South America to North America.

We began to see a whole new tragedy unfold. The cocaine hydrochloride was passing through in such enormous quantities that the spillage created a massive cocaine problem. The simple process of cooking this powder with baking soda from the supermarket released the chloride ion and made a cocaine crystal which was about ninety percent pure. It was called *freebase* back then, and it was only years later that the term *crack* was introduced.

We saw a peaceful society decimated by violence, crime and quick cash. The false economy thrived and far too many of society's decision makers chose to look the other way. The situation worsened and the public seemed indifferent to the warnings of the professionals.

The authors have treated many people for addictions (we have written about this in a previous chapter). They were on the cutting edge of knowledge, especially about cocaine, which we began experiencing in 1973, and which became a full blown epidemic by 1983.

There were many workshops in the Bahamas warning the world about the devastation of this so-called 'recreational' drug. We warned about the impending consequence of serious societal problems *viz. a viz.* transport, trafficking, drug pushing and cocaine addiction. Yet, there were many in the USA who thought that we 'Island Boys' didn't know what we were talking about. Tim reacted immediately to an article written in the *Miami Herald,* July 11, 1990 by Arnold S. Trebach, director of the Institute on Drugs, Crime, and Justice of the American University, Washington, D.C. The letter follows:

Bahamian warning of 'crack' dangers

To the editor:

I read with horror an article in the July 11 *Herald* by Arnold S. Trebach, director of the Institute on Drugs, Crime, and Justice of the American University, Washington D.C.

Trebach has expressed doubts as to the "addictiveness" and "effects" of cocaine, and he is hesitant to label as an "epidemic" the cocaine situation in America. His lack of knowledge of cocaine and its effects is pathetic!

We in the Bahamas have had to deal with freebase cocaine – "rocks," "nuggets," or as Americans call it "crack" – for the past seven years. In the Bahamas, the method began to take hold in Florida initially in November, 1985, and then in California.

Our experience has shown that:

- Cocaine is the most highly addictive illegal drug available at present.

- The unpredictability of the action of crack on the body places the user in a highly susceptible situation for heart attack, stroke, seizures, or cocaine psychosis.

- Crack addiction in any community is usually accompanied by an escalation of crime, prostitution, and sexually transmitted illnesses.

- Crack kills!

We have developed some expertise in prevention and treatment programs and will be happy to share our knowledge, as we did recently at an international conference here when Dr. Washton from the U.S.A. and experts from England, the Caribbean, and South America shared experiences.

Professor Trebach would do his Institute and the American people a service by becoming more knowledgeable of cocaine and refraining from writing confusing and inaccurate articles. I predict that cocaine abuse will probably become endemic in America within the next year.

Timothy McCartney
Department of Psychology,
Sandilands Rehabilitation Centre,
Ministry of Health,
Nassau, Bahamas

———

In March 1983, having followed in Tim's footsteps as President of the Bahamas Mental Health Association, Mike spoke on radio shows and wrote in the newspapers. The public reaction was amply demonstrated when Mike's efforts were lampooned in a classic cartoon by Burnside suggesting he should calm down.

Nassau Guardian, March 25, 1983

He also gave evidence during the 1984 Commission of Inquiry into Drug Trafficking. He stated that cocaine presented a massive danger, but the threat was largely ignored. The observer, Mr. David Stockley, sent by Scotland Yard to assist the commission was very concerned, but he could not get the warning out either. He later wrote to Mike stating that neither the Department of Health nor the European police took us seriously. They felt "it was just a cultural thing in the Caribbean."

Tim and Mike were also very involved in many other societal issues, including women's conferences. Both were speakers at a number of vibrant events. Tim's daughter Angela was one of the organizers and Tim even discussed the possibility of male pregnancy. At about the same time Mike's wife, Sandra started the first women's desk in the Bahamas. She was attempting to sensitize the public on gender issues and again the public reaction perceived such talk as threatening, as you can see in another classic cartoon by Sideburns.

The sad reality is that these problems are still pressing today. Cocaine has spread to become a scourge around the world, and now everyone is an expert, but nothing changes.

The issues of gender inequality still rumble around the world, with brave new laws, but only lip service to their implementation. Rape and child abuse in all its forms make great headlines, but lead to limited convictions.

The world is changing rapidly in front of our eyes and the drum beat of opposition to change is growing ever stronger with calls to censor the internet, concerns about the impact of violent games, and even the damage caused by social networks.

There is much less discussion on the enormous benefits to social change that could be brought about by this wireless phenomenon that will soon be driving the whole world. It is still not necessary to reinvent the wheel. Whatever problem you as an individual are facing can be researched at the touch of a keypad.

This is just as true for societal problems. Whatever situation a country may be facing, it is very simple to find out what other countries and cities have faced and find out what works and what does not. The buzz word in modern medicine is *evidence-based*. It is no longer accepted that things can be done the way we always did it. Now there must be proper research showing that an approach works successfully.

———

Births, weddings and funerals are often the cornerstone of family life. These events usually bring us all together; and, if it is someone that people feel is really important, we could extrapolate that to the whole of society.

These events can even bring us all together. How the event is staged varies from culture to culture, but the common ground of a special ceremony is designed to strengthen the family. The Bahamas takes funerals very seriously: large, long and lavish could describe an important laying to rest ceremony. The coffin begins the service open and is closed with mass hysteria during the service. The procession to the graveside is accompanied by bands playing the family's choice of music. With finality of the lowering of the casket comes a final goodbye.

In rural Ireland where our forebears are from, there are certain similarities. The coffin is accepted into the church the night before the interment. The family returns to the house to talk about the deceased and some fine Irish whiskey is downed. The next morning it is off to church for the Mass for the Dead, and then the lowering into the grave. Both countries have lavish get-togethers for family and friends after the interment, when the mood is usually lighter, but moods can oscillate from laughter to arguments and fights.

In England, the land of the stiff upper lip, a funeral may well be one car behind the hearse on the way to the crematorium on a Monday morning. No tears, no grief, even no fights. The difference occurs years after the loss of a loved one. The cardiac clinic, the gastroenterology clinic and, yes, the mental health clinics are inhabited by patients who never expressed their grief. That negative energy has boiled over, creating very real sickness.

In cultures where opportunities for the expression of grief are accepted this atypical lack of grief is less common. This is not a panacea for society's ills, but it does remind us that as we strive for newer and better ways of solving problems, there is sometimes good reason for the old traditional ways. If the evidence shows that the old ways work well, do not change just for change's sake.

There is a possible game-changing moment looming ahead of us. We must start to use the communicating potential of the new wireless world to break down barriers just like social media helped with the Arab spring. The stigma and perceived shame of mental illness, domestic violence and child abuse can finally have the illumination of knowledge shone upon them. We have known for a long time that by breaking the code of silence, many of these problems can be stopped and prevented.

We envisage not the potential horrors of the brave new world of oppression by surveillance, but the ability to share information – to open up the dreaded secrets of family abuse, of bullies, of substance abuse. We know that when these issues are talked about openly they stop! We now have the tools to shine the light of information on so many things and finally throw away the shackles of the stigma attached to mental illness.

We have lived to see far too many predictions come true. It would almost be nice to be wrong.

BIBLIOGRAPHY

REFERENCES

Cannon, Walter B. (1932) *The Wisdom Of The Body.* W.W. Norton, New York.

Ellis, A. (1963). *Reason and Emotion in Psychotherapy.* New York: Lyle Stuart Inc.

Eysenck, Haus J. (1988). *Health's Character Psychology Today,* p. 28-35. USA.

Forisha, Barbara L. (1978). *Sex Roles and Personal Awareness.* Morristown, New Jersey: General Learning Press.

Freud, S. (1950). Collected Papers.

Gibson, J. L., Ivancevich, J. M., Donnelly, J. H. (Jr.) and Konopaske, R. (2012). *Organizations: Behavior, Structure, Processes.* New York, NY: McGraw-Hill/Irwin.

Gould, Roger (1972). *The Seasons of a Man's Life.* Toronto, Canada: Ballantine Books of Canada.

Greenberg, J.S. (1993). *Comprehensive Stress Management.* Brown and Benchmark: Dubuque, Iowa.

Hersey, P. and Campbell, R. (2004). *Leadership: A Behavioral Science Approach.* Center for Leadership Studies, California (USA). ISBN: 0-931619-09-2.

Levinson, Daniel, et al. (1978). *The Seasons of a Man's Life.* Toronto, Canada: Ballantine Books of Canada.

Lewis, M. and Weinraub, M. (1974). *Sex of Parent and Sex of Child: Socio-Emotional Development.*

McCartney, T. and Neville, M. (1998). *The Therapeutic Learning Process as Effective Modality in Coping with Addictions OD Intervention.* Borco, Freeport, Grand Bahama, Bahamas.

MacCoby, E. E., and Jacklin, C. (1974). *The Psychology of Sex Differences*. Standford, CA: Stanford University Press.

Maultsby, Maxie C. (1984). *Rational Behavior Therapy*. Englewood Cliffs, New Jersey: Prentice-Hall.

Mujtaba, B.G. (2008). *Coaching and Performance Management: Developing and Inspiring Leaders*. Davie, FL, USA: ILEAD Academy Publications.

Mujtaba, B. G. and McCartney, T. O. (2010) *Managing Workplace Stress and Conflict Amid Change*. (2nd ed.). Davie, FL, USA: ILEAD Academy Publications.

Rogers, C. R. and Roethlisberger, F. J. (1952). *Barriers and Gateways to Communication*. Harvard Business Review.

Rokeach, M. (1986). *Beliefs, Attitudes and Values: A Theory of Organization and Changes*. San Francisco, CA: Jossey-Bass Publishers.

Seyle, H. (1956). *The Stress of Life*. New York, New York: McGraw-Hill Books Co.

Sheehy, G. (1976). *Passages: Predictable Crises of Adult Life*. New York, New York: E.P. Dutton and Company Inc.

Vaillant, George E. and McArthur, Charles C. (1972). *Natural History of Male Psychologic Health: The Adult Life Cycle From 18-50*. Seminars in Psychiatry 4(4).

Williams, Mackey. (2010) *McPherson Street and The Folks Who Lived There: A Captivating Evolution*, PO Box N-1316, Nassau, Bahamas.

AUTHOR BIOGRAPHIES

Timothy McCartney is a Distinguished Professor of Management and the Paul Hersey Chair in Leadership and Organizational Behavior at the H. Wayne Huizenga School of Business and Entrepreneurship, Nova Southeastern University, Fort Lauderdale, Florida.

He is a Clinical Psychologist and also an Organizational Development Consultant, facilitating seminars, workshops and advising national and multinational companies in the Caribbean and worldwide.

Dr. McCartney was educated in the Bahamas. USA, Switzerland, Jamaica, England, and France where he obtained a Doctorate in Clinical Psychology – "tres honorable!" (*Summa cum laude*). He has received many awards and citations for his contribution to psychology and mental health from national and international communities. He has obtained *Excellence in Teaching* Awards and was named *Students' Choice Professor of the Year*, 2008/2009.

Dr. McCartney is married to Pauline and they have four children (one is deceased), eighteen grandchildren, and eight great grands.

―――――

Dr. Michael Neville received his medical degree at the Royal College of Surgeons, Dublin, Ireland in 1973. He interned at Princess Margaret Hospital, in the Bahamas and worked for a year in the emergency room.

Dr. Neville then trained as a psychiatrist in Manchester, England where he received a Diploma in Psychological Medicine and the Membership of the Royal College of Psychiatrists. He returned to the Bahamas in 1979 and has worked as a Consultant Psychiatrist at Sandilands Rehabilitation and at Doctor's Hospital.

Dr. Neville has a special interest in forensic psychiatry and has worked at Fox Hill Prison and given expert testimony to the courts in both civil and criminal matters. He has conducted research and has published numerous papers and has presented his work at many conferences. He served on the country's Prison Commission and on the last Crime Council. He has a special interest in *why* people commit murder.

He has been awarded the Member of the British Empire (MBE) by Queen Elizabeth and the medal *Pro Ecclesia et Pontifice* by Pope John Paul II; both medals for his services in mental health to the people of the Bahamas.

Dr. Neville is married to Sandra. They have three children and four grandchildren.

———